D1826644

New Designs in
Lace Making

KRISTINA MALMBERG

NAIME THORLIN

VNR VAN NOSTRAND REINHOLD COMPANY
New York   Cincinnati   Toronto   London   Melbourne

Van Nostrand Reinhold Company Regional
Offices:
New York   Cincinnati   Chicago   Millbrae
Dallas
Van Nostrand Reinhold Company International
Offices:
London   Toronto   Melbourne

This book was originally published in Sweden
under the title *Knyppla, Idéer och modeller
i nya och kända material* by ICA-förlaget AB.

Copyright © 1973 for *Knyppla*
by ICA-förlaget AB
English copyright © 1974 Van Nostrand
Reinhold Company Ltd.

Translated from the Swedish by Lotta Juhlin

Library of Congress Catalog Card Number:
74-5941
ISBN 0–442–30050–6 (cl)
ISBN 0–442–30051–4 (pb)

Photography by Sven-Erik Sjöström, Reteam
Foto

This book is set in Univers,
printed by Jolly and Barber Ltd., Rugby,
and bound by Webb, Son and Company,
Ferndale, Glamorgan.

Published by Van Nostrand Reinhold
Company Inc.,
450 West 33rd Street, New York N.Y. 10001 and
Van Nostrand Reinhold Company Ltd.,
Molly Millar's Lane, Wokingham, Berkshire.

16 15 14 13 12 11 10 9 8 7 6 5 4 3 2 1

**Library of Congress Cataloging in Publication
Data**
Malmberg, Kristina, 1932–
    New designs in lacemaking.
    (Reinhold craft paperback)
    Translation of Knyppla. Idéer och modeller
inya och kända material.
    1. Bobbin lace – Patterns. I. Thorlin, Naime,
joint author. II. Title.
TT805.M3413   746.2′2   74–5941
ISBN 0–442–30050–6
ISBN 0–442–30051–4 (pbk.)

Contents

Introduction

The beautiful and intricate designs of traditional lace making can be seen in many art galleries and museums of costume, but variations on these patterns can also be used very effectively to fit in with modern requirements and tastes in dress, textiles, and decoration.

The aim of this book is to demonstrate different practical ways to use lace. Each chapter offers both familiar techniques and new materials, methods, and functions.

The various laces are described in detail and illustrated by photographs and drawings which clarify the patterns and the procedures. Many suggestions are offered for further applications of the laces and for alterations in the designs and the materials.

This book is intended for lace makers who already know the basics, but a chapter has been included that repeats the most common stitches and grounds. The ideas presented here will inspire the reader to continue the development of lace, either along traditional lines or in completely free directions.

1. Materials, tools, and procedures

Fig. 1–1. New and familiar materials.

Laces are traditionally made with very fine white threads; there is scarcely any information available on working with coarse or coloured materials. These materials are not only much easier to use, but also they suggest many exciting new possibilities. This book presents a range of different patterns which utilize a variety of natural materials.

Before selecting the material for a given lace it is important to determine the function of the finished article. If it is to be used primarily for decoration it need not be as strong as an article that will be washed and ironed a lot. Cotton and wool are suitable for the latter case.

The most commonly used natural materials are cotton yarn no. 8/4, weaving linen and linen thread no. 16/2, and two-ply worsted wool yarn. You may substitute other yarns of the same coarseness, however, and alternatives are suggested in the pattern instructions. The new materials covered in this book are strips of fabric or leather, different kinds of string, velvet ribbons, fishing line, and linen and cotton carpet thread.

All lace makers are familiar with the ordinary tools like pillows, bobbins, pins, and the spool machine; they do not need any further introduction. There are, however, some rather unconventional tools that might come in handy:

1. A square of polystyrene or hardboard 20 × 20 in. (50 × 50 cm.) makes a splendid pillow for larger laces. If the square feels too light you can anchor it with a brick covered in velours.

2. Many of these new coarser materials must be fastened with a stronger pin than the ordinary fine pin.

3. Some of the laces need chequered fabrics in addition to the usual patterns pinned on pricking cards. (If the pattern is only a sketch you can draw it on tracing paper supported by a pricking card.)

4. It is easier to pin on the pattern if you fix the pricking card and the square-ruled paper between a pair of prickers.

5. You will need larger bobbins than usual for coarser materials. You can store them by crocheting a suitably long chain of woollen yarn. Then reverse direction, crocheting half-trebles in every other link, and fasten the ends together. Since the wool is elastic it is easy to slip the bobbins through the holes to keep them in order.

You should sit properly in a well-lit position while working. Your chair and table should stand at a comfortable height, and you should have enough room round the pillow for fabric and tools.

The approximate time necessary to complete the lace is provided for many of the patterns. This includes only the actual lace making, so you should also estimate the hours spent in deciding on a project and obtaining the materials if the total length of time required is an important consideration.

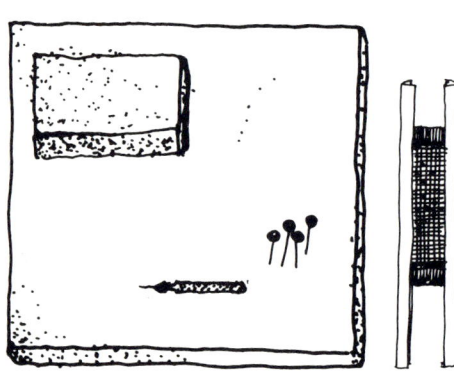

Fig. 1–2. a. A hardboard lace pillow with a brick, coarse pins, and a pricker. b. A useful arrangement for pinning up the pattern.

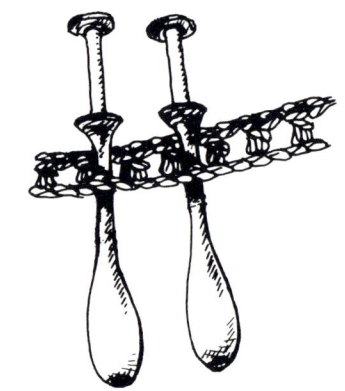

Fig. 1–3. A crocheted ribbon with holes to keep bobbins in order.

2. Laces for interior decoration

By introducing new materials you can extend the uses of lace to include quite large household articles. Actually the word 'lace' is not comprehensive enough to describe these patterns; they should be called 'lace works'.

Striped curtain

Laces large enough for interior decoration can be produced with strips of fabric. You do not have to draw a pattern or shift continuously among different grounds; on the contrary, it is preferable to use a single tight ground which emphasizes the material and the colours. If you work on a loose ground you will have to stitch the finished lace on to a stabilizing piece of fabric.

Stretch strips of chequered fabric on a square of hardboard. If the lace is to be long you will need a reel fixed in a wooden frame. The reel should be placed at the edge of a table so that the strips will hang straight. The difference between the vertical technique and the horizontal one is that in the former the strips are pinned as soon as a pair of bobbins is introduced.

Use cotton remnants (which are inexpensive) for the curtains. Before cutting the fabric into strips it should be washed so that it is soft and easy to work with. The curtain in fig. 2–1 is stretched between two wooden hangers and hung on a pine wall.
Material: Strips of twill-weave cotton; 72 pairs of bobbins.

Colour chart:

red	orange	yellow
12 pairs	6 pairs	8 pairs
pale yellow	yellow	
6 pairs	4 pairs	
red	pale yellow	orange
10 pairs	6 pairs	4 pairs
yellow	red	
6 pairs	10 pairs	

Technique: Double cloth stitches.
Size: 26 × 80 in. (65 × 200 cm.)
Pattern: The lace is made on a reel 32 in. (80 cm.) wide. (See the drawing, fig. 2–4.) The reel is covered by chequered fabric with $\frac{3}{4}$ in. (1·8 cm.) squares that serves as a pattern.
Procedure: Cut the fabric in strips $\frac{3}{4}$ in. (1·8 cm.) wide, slanting the ends. Join the ends either by stitching or machine-

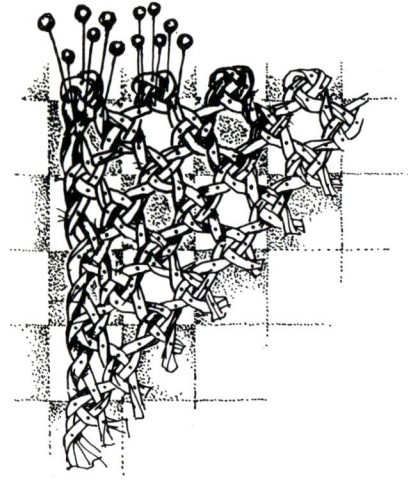

Fig. 2–2. To get enough stability at the beginning, put four pins in each stitch through the crossing, the twist, the crossing, and the twist.

Fig. 2–5. Left and right. The reel set up with cotton remnants.

Opposite. Fig. 2–1. Striped curtain, designed and executed by Ingegerd Gyrulf. See colour plate 8, opposite p. 64.

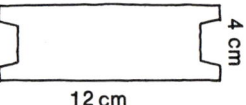

Fig. 2–3. Cut out pieces of pasteboard measuring 1½ × 4¾ in. (3·6 × 1·4 cm.), and wind the strips round these.

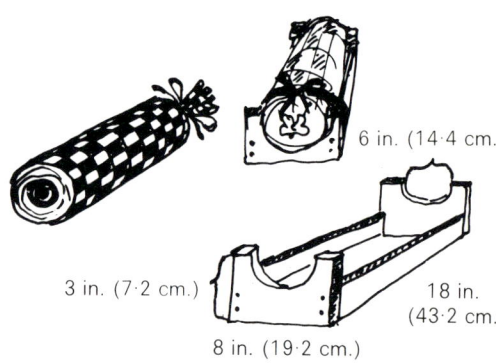

Fig. 2–4. You can make a reel yourself from pasteboard and felt. Roll up the pasteboard, and tape the ends together with broad parcel tape. Cover the reel with three or four layers of felt, and fasten both ends with textile glue. Fix a chequered fabric on top of the felt. You can also construct a lace making trestle yourself (see p. 93), or order it from a carpenter. Reel frame. 3 in. (7·2 cm.), 8 in. (19·2 cm.), 6 in. (14·4 cm.), 18 in. (43·2 cm.).

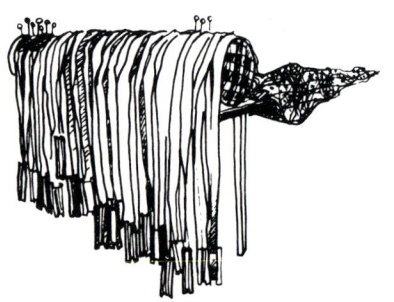

sewing them. The length of the strips should be about three times the length of the finished curtain. Wind the strips on pieces of pasteboard as shown in the sketch, fig. 2–5, and fasten them with pins. Double each strip, and roll the pairs inward from the ends. When estimating the width and the number of strips remember that they will contract by 10% after the pins are removed.

Start by fastening two pairs of bobbins at the border of each square with double cloth stitches, moving diagonally from right to left. Stick pins through the second twist in each stitch. You do not need extra twists in the braid.

Work the pairs diagonally over the lace, constantly changing the colours to highlight the attractive square pattern. If the stripes are begun asymmetrically the squares will also become asymmetrical.

When the work is finished cut off three strips close to the last stitch, and secure them with a few stitches. Cut one strip ¾ in. (1·8 cm.) longer than the rest, fold it over backwards, and fasten it to the other strips.

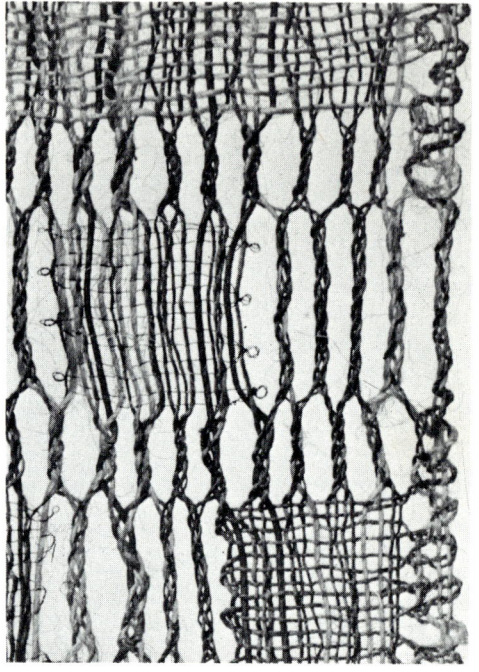

Fig. 2–6. Hemp string tapestry (detail), designed and executed by Ingegerd Gyrulf.

Hemp string tapestry

This lace is made from rather rough materials, but they are well-suited for interior decoration. The tapestry can be used to divide a room or a hallway.

Material: Jute, hemp, and paper strings; 30 pairs of bobbins; copper thread; 1 pair of bobbins.

Technique: Cloth stitch, net, and torchon grounds; plaits of different lengths.

Pattern: The lace is made on a reel fixed in a wooden frame and covered with chequered fabric.

Fig. 2–7. Here the copper threads have become the workers. Make a loop round the pin when turning.

Fig. 2–9. Details of the string-work in the lace.

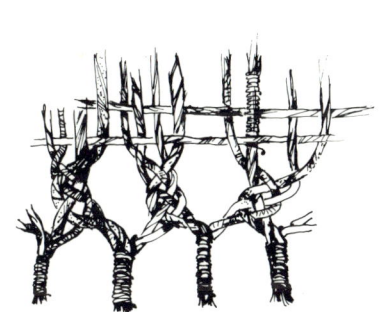

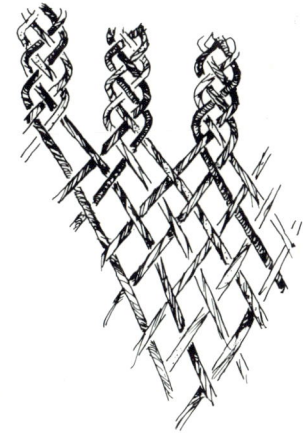

Fig. 2–8. To finish-off, wind the copper thread round the string.

Fig. 2–10. Plaits that dissolve into a net.

Border

This coarse lace in linen warp is made freely on a chequered fabric even though the pattern is symmetrical. The drawing is transferred to a traditional paper pattern. The design is reproduced in full scale on $\frac{1}{4}$ in. (6 mm.) square-ruled paper in fig. 2–12.

Material: Unbleached linen warp no. 8/4; 24 pairs of bobbins; unbleached linen warp no. 8/4 plyed four times for contouring; 1 pair of bobbins.

Technique: Cloth stitch; net ground; torchon ground with twists; gimp.

Size: The entire lace is $5\frac{3}{4}$ in. (14 cm.) wide; each complete section of the pattern is $3\frac{1}{2}$ in. (8·4 cm.) long.

Pattern: The pattern is drawn full scale on $\frac{1}{4}$ in. (6 mm.) square-ruled paper.

Procedure: Spool the bobbins together, setting up the pairs in accordance with the drawing, fig. 2–12. Begin with torchon ground with twists and cloth stitches at the edges. Bring in the gimp. Then make the centre square with torchon ground and cloth stitches. Note that the pairs that enter or leave the cloth stitch ground should always be twisted twice, except when moving from cloth stitch to torchon ground at the edges. Continue torchon ground at the edges parallel to the centre square. Complete the two net grounds before advancing to the next section. Twist the workers twice when they turn in the corner of the cloth stitch ground, as in the detailed photograph, fig. 2–11.

Fig. 2–11. Border, a coarse lace in linen warp designed and executed by Elin Abrahamsson.

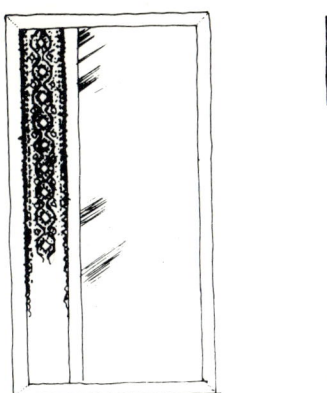
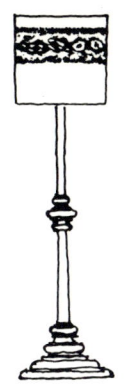

Fig. 2–13. The lace can be fitted on a mirror or round a rustic lampshade.

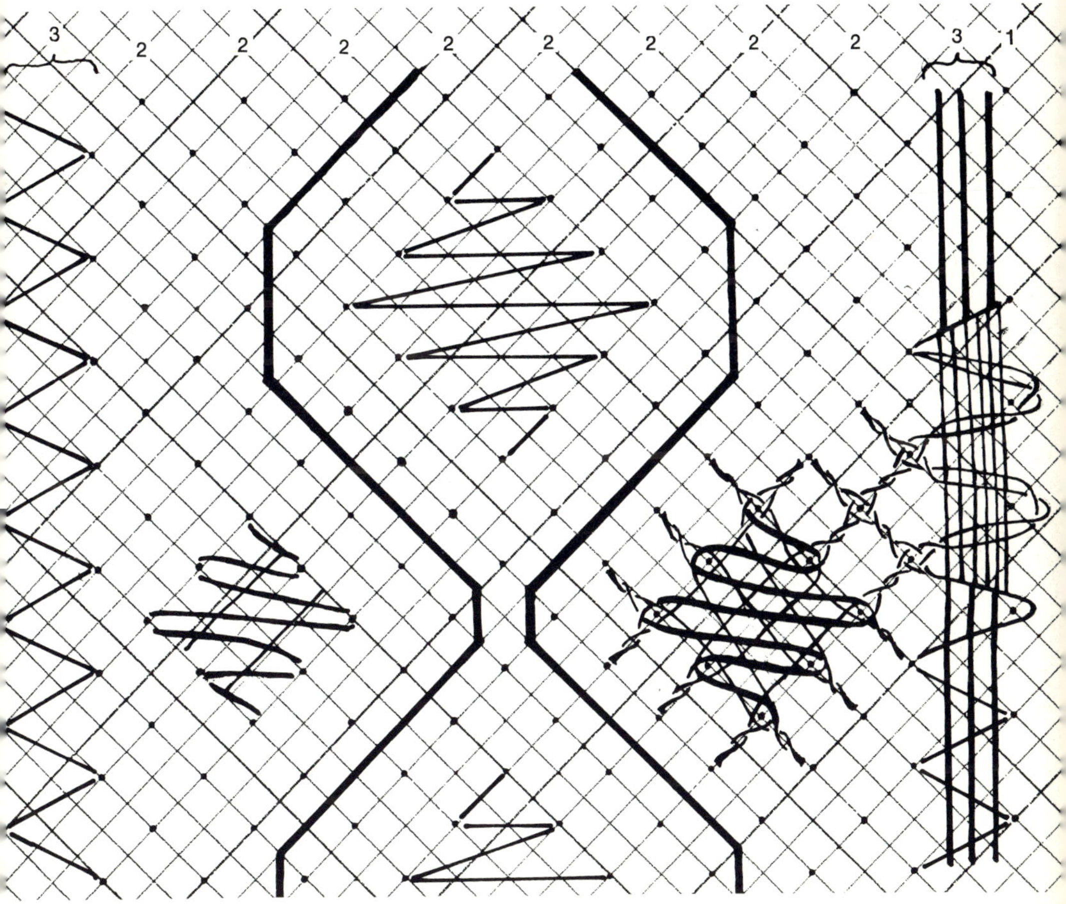

Fig. 2–12. Pattern drawing. The digits indicate the number of pairs.

Fig. 2–14. Lace of hearts, designed and executed by Signe Wahlström.

Lace of hearts

You can enlarge a pattern, use a coarser thread, and extend the use of a lace if you are skilled enough and have a good sense for proportions. This shelf lace was originally thin and complicated, but now is much simpler and faster to make, and also serves a new purpose.

Material: Semi-bleached weft yarn no. 18/5; 14 pairs of bobbins; unbleached linen yarn no. 16/2 (four threads spooled together); 1 bobbin.
Technique: Cloth stitch ground; torchon ground with twists; gimp.
Size: The entire lace is 3 in. (7·2 cm.) wide. Each complete section of the pattern is $2\frac{3}{4}$ in. (6·6 cm.) long.
Pattern: The pattern is drawn in full scale on $\frac{1}{4}$ in. (6 mm.) square-ruled paper.
Procedure: Start the lace as shown in the drawing, fig. 2–17, with a double cloth stitch in the point. Bring in the gimp, and make a cloth stitch through two pairs, giving an extra twist to the workers when turning. Continue with cloth stitches towards the point; bring in the gimp again; and make the point with double cloth stitch, extra twist, pin, and double cloth stitch. Thereafter twist the passives once. Finish making the cloth stitch square with loose edges, and put the gimp round the entire figure, in accordance with the photograph and the drawing, figs. 2–14 and 15.

Pass to the cloth stitch ground, the heart. Hang first two pairs of bobbins round the gimp before making the first cloth stitch, as shown in the detail, fig. 2–16 a and b. Then make a half-stitch inside the braid with these two pairs. Pass one of the pairs through the gimp into the cloth stitch ground; and move the other pair over the braid with double cloth stitch, extra twist, pin, and double cloth stitch. When half the heart is finished, make a torchon ground with twist and braid on the left-hand side, as shown on the drawing, fig. 2–17. On the right-hand side make a plait with double cloth stitch, pin, double

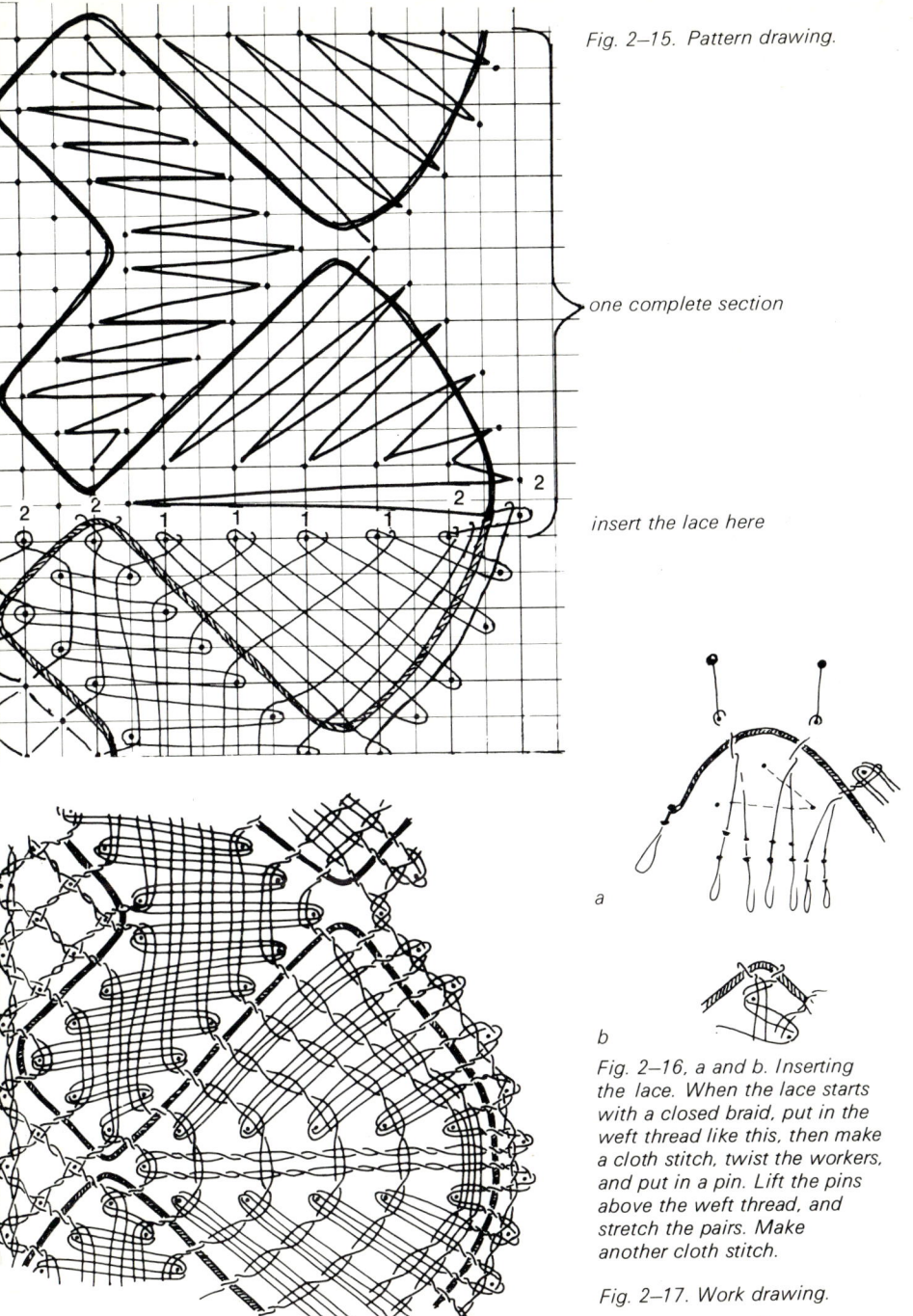

Fig. 2–15. Pattern drawing.

one complete section

insert the lace here

a

b

Fig. 2–16, a and b. Inserting the lace. When the lace starts with a closed braid, put in the weft thread like this, then make a cloth stitch, twist the workers, and put in a pin. Lift the pins above the weft thread, and stretch the pairs. Make another cloth stitch.

Fig. 2–17. Work drawing.

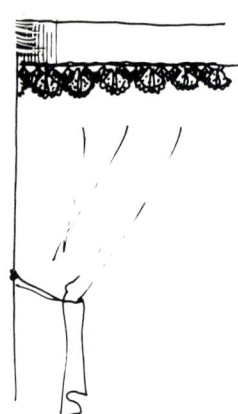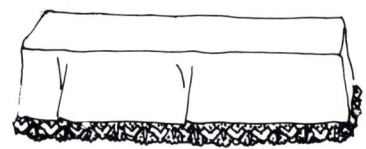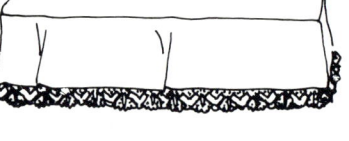

Fig. 2–18. Ways of using the lace.

cloth stitch. Work the second half of the heart in the same way as the first but in reversed order.

Fitting: Stitch the lace on a folded linen ribbon. Thread an elastic ribbon through the linen ribbon, and stretch it against the edge of a shelf. Fix both ends to the shelf with drawing pins.

Bead fringe for curtains

Material: Lace yarn no. 15/3 or linen yarn no. 16/2; 8 pairs of bobbins; glass or wooden beads $\frac{1}{4}$ in. (6 mm.) in diameter (10 beads for every 4 in. (9·6 cm.) of fabric).

Technique: Plaits.

Size: The fringe with beads is about 1$\frac{3}{4}$ in. (4·2 cm.) wide. One complete section of the pattern is $\frac{1}{2}$ in. (1·2 cm.) long.

Procedure: Spool the pairs of bobbins together two by two. For the beads, spool half of one bobbin with yarn, then fill the rest with beads. (The bobbin will hold about ten at a time.) The lace consists only of plaits: the method is cloth stitch, stretch, twist, cross, stretch, etc. The drawing does not show the number of stitches since you must decide how much to stretch. (Test how many stitches are needed for the various distances, stretching continuously.) Bring in the bobbin with the beads outside the pin in the point, and feed the beads into the lace at the point. Roll up the thread, and slip on more beads as you go along. Follow the drawing, fig. 2–20, for best results. The following two designs are variations on the fringe theme.

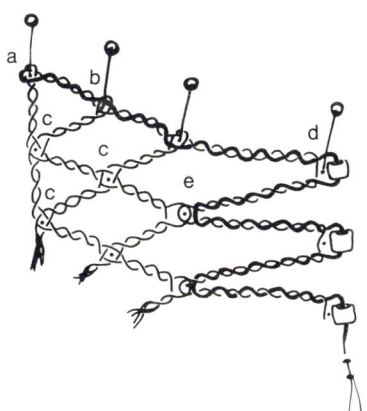

*Fig. 2–19. Bead fringe for
curtains, designed
by Birgitta Rudeskog and
executed by Signe Andersson.*

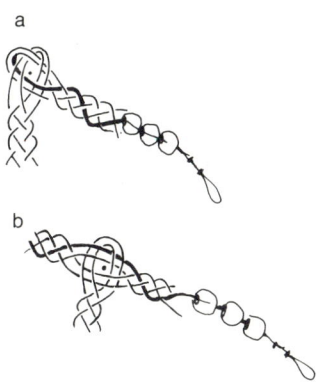

*Fig. 2–20. Bead fringes: For bead fringe for
curtains, hang four plaited pairs on the first
pin. A single bobbin carries the beads; its path
is marked with a dark line in the drawings.
(a.) Make the stitch, using each pair as one*

*bobbin: Cross, twist, pin, cross. Make the
plaits with separate threads: Cross, twist, cross,
stretch, twist, cross, stretch, etc. (b.) Finish the
plait with a crossing, and bring in two new
pairs here and at the following pin. Make the*

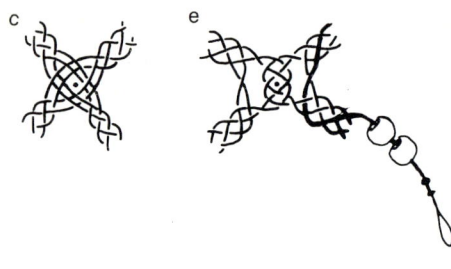

stitch as in a. (c.) Finish the plait stitches with a crossing, stretching them well. Be sure that there is enough room round the pin to put the four pairs together and to make the stitch as in a. (di.) Finish the plait with a twist. The bead thread should be far to the right. Put the pin in the centre. There should be two threads on each side of the pin when you leave the beads in the point. (dii.) Place the bead in the point, twisting the bead bobbin over the nearest thread to the left. Make a cloth stitch, and push the bead as near to the pin as possible. Continue the plait. (e.) Finish the plaits with a twist. Make a double cloth stitch with the two inner pairs. Put down a pin, and make another double cloth stitch. Continue the plaiting. The bead bobbin goes out to the point again. For round bead fringe for curtains, hang four pairs of bobbins together on the first pin. The bead bobbin is marked with a thick black line. Hang two pairs on the second pin. The thread with beads is marked with a double line.
(fi.) Put down a pin as in d. Plait three threads the same length as the bead. (fii.) Push up the bead, and put down a pin. Twist the bead bobbin over the nearest thread, and continue the plaiting.

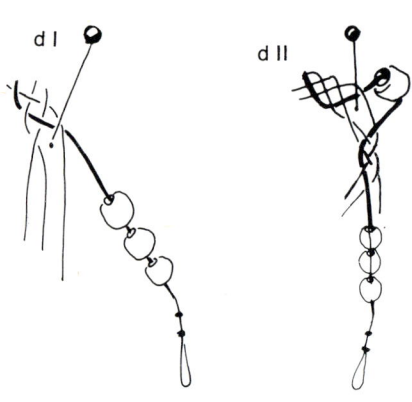

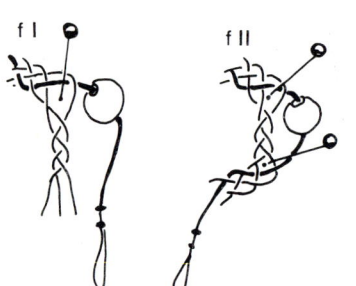

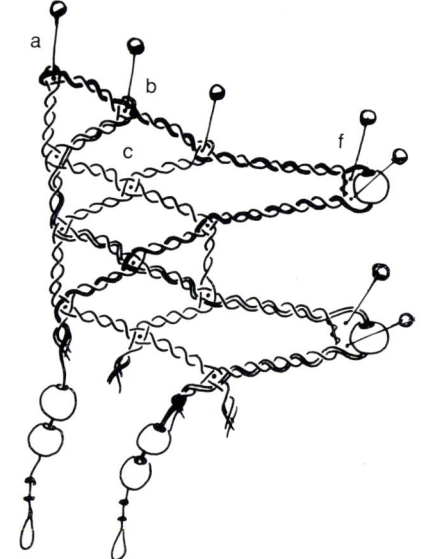

Fig. 2–21. A lace like this round bead fringe, designed by Birgitta Rudeskog and executed by Signe Andersson, is very useful for decorating clothes and interiors. It can be thin or coarse, depending on how it is used.

Round bead fringe for curtains

Material: Linen warp no. 8/3 or 8/2: 8 pairs of bobbins: wooden beads $\frac{3}{8}$ in. (9 mm.) in diameter (5 beads for every 4 in. (9·6 cm.) of fabric).

Technique: Plaits.

Size: The fringe with beads is about $2\frac{1}{2}$ in. (6 cm.) wide. One complete section of the pattern is about $\frac{3}{4}$ in. (1·8 cm.) long.

Procedure: This lace requires two bobbins for the beads, which go out to the point alternately. The work sketch, fig. 2–20, f 1 and 2, shows how to bring them in. Note that the plaits in the points (where the beads are placed) are made with three threads.

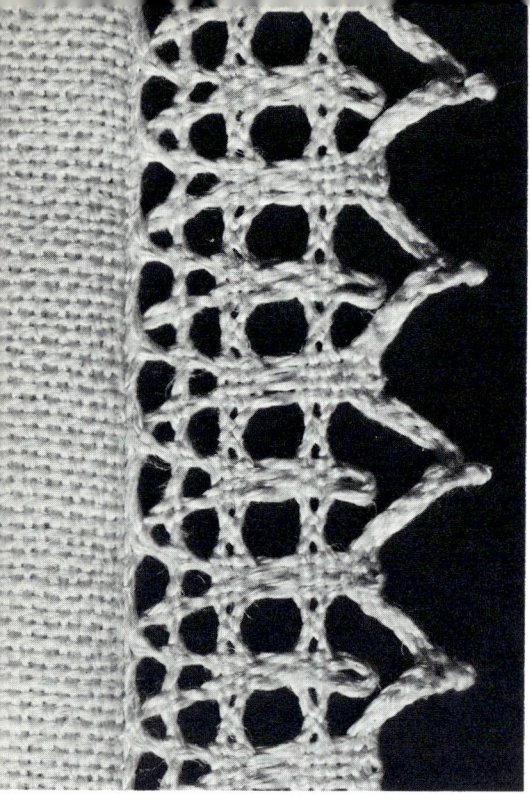

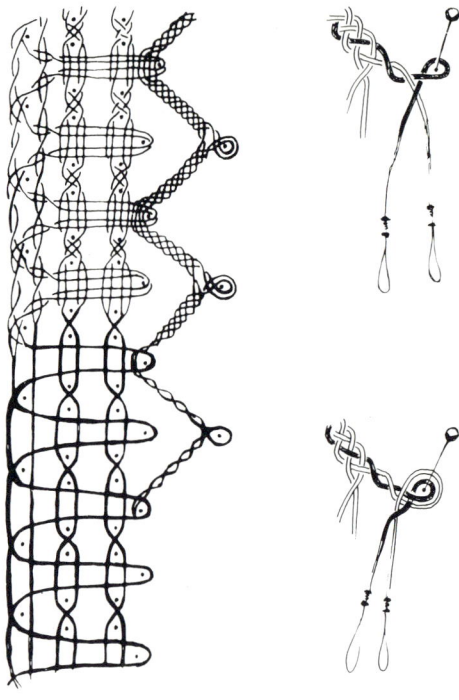

Fig. 2–22. Playing brownies, designed by Britta Torstensson and executed by Marta Nilsson.

Fig. 2–23. Work drawing. The lower part shows a simpler variation without plaits and picot.

Fig. 2–24. How to make the picot.

Playing brownies

Material: Weft yarn no. 18/3; 9 pairs of bobbins.

Technique: Cloth stitches: double cloth stitches: plaits: picot.

Size: The lace is about 1¼ in. (3 cm.) wide. One complete section of the pattern is ¾ in. (1·8 cm.) long.

Procedure: Put up the pairs of bobbins as shown in the work sketch, fig. 2–23. Make cloth stitches through the six pairs on the right, pin, twist the workers, and return through the six pairs with cloth stitches. Then make a closed braid with double cloth stitch, double cloth stitch, extra twist, pin, double cloth stitch. Twist the four passives from the cloth stitch ground,

supporting the loop with a pin, then make a double cloth stitch round the pin. (See the drawing, fig. 2–24.)

Move to the plait on the right-hand side; cross, twist, cross, stretch, twist, cross, stretch, etc., repeating this sequence until you reach the pin, and finish-off with a twist. Twist the outer pair once again, then make a picot with the thread that is nearest to the point, as in the photograph, fig. 2–22. Lay the second thread round the pin, and twist once. Continue the picot in the same manner. Make the inner part of the lace with enough cloth stitches to set off the border design clearly. (This lace can be simplified by omitting the plait and the picot.)

3. Decorative laces

Naturally, decorative laces are used differently from household laces. The picture laces in this chapter are presented quite loosely to allow individual interpretation of both material and pattern. Some of them need only the usual pricked pattern, while others require an additional drawing.

Luna

This is a fully laced motif inspired by the latest photographs from the moon. The lace is described in detail in the drawing, fig. 3–2. (The pattern may be varied by adding or subtracting a twist, depending on your personal style.)

Material: Unbleached linen yarn no. 16/2; 44 pairs of bobbins; 1 extra pair of bobbins in the middle of the work.

Technique: Cloth stitch ground; plaits.

Size: 8 in. × 8 in. (20 × 20 cm.).

Procedure: The motif starts and finishes with a closed braid. Put three pairs, the workers and two passives, on the first pin to the left; put one pair on the second pin, etc. Put two pairs on the first pin to the right. (Note that the worker passes round the pin with cloth stitch.)

The drawing of the middle of the lace, fig. 3–2, shows both threads in the pair. The loose part of the pattern will help you to determine the appropriate number of twists necessary to give the lace the right spacy look. In the surrounding cloth stitch ground each pair is indicated by one line, with the exception of certain details in which both threads are shown to make the pattern clearer.

Insert the extra pair at the location marked by the sign ∩, and remove it where the sign ╳ appears, as shown in the detailed sketch, fig. 3–3. The cloth stitches should be very firm.

The finishing braid is completed as follows: after the workers have travelled through all the passives from right to left, pass them round the last pin to the left. Twist them once, make a cloth stitch, and pass them back through four pairs. Lay them aside for the moment, but do not cut off the threads until the lace is finished. The two adjoining passives to the left lie between the first and the second pinholes. Twist both pairs once, pass them through the following four pairs with cloth stitches, then remove them from the work. Twist the third passive once. Put the

21

Fig. 3–1. Luna, designed by Kasja Borg and executed by Signe Andersson.

pin in the second pin-hole, make a cloth stitch round the pin, and let the third passive pass through four pairs. Follow the same procedure with the rest of the passives.

Pin the last three pairs on the right to the lace, as explained in the section on finishing-off in Chapter 9. Cut these threads off, allowing 2–4 in. (5–10 cm.) to remain. Cut the rest of the threads close while they are still pinned to the lace.

Fitting: Fasten the two upper corners of the lace with thin nylon thread so that the fitting is as invisible as possible.

Fig. 3–2. Work drawing.

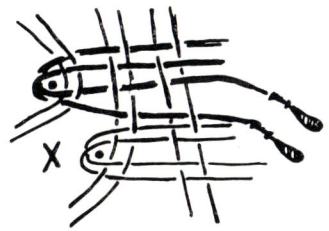

Fig. 3–3. Detail of the lace work. Instead of simply tying away a pair you can remove them in this manner, which is more suitable for a loose lace.

X

Modus vivendi

Fig. 3–4. Pattern
and work drawing
in full scale. Each
line represents a
pair.

This is a purely decorative lace that combines thick and thin threads with knots to create a random effect.

Material: Cotton warp no. 12/6; linen warp no. 8/5; linen thread no. 28/4; linen yarn or lace thread no. 25/3, 40/2, or 18/5; tow yarn for rings; hand-spun linen yarn; linen-effect yarn; linen yarn no. 28/4 or 16/2 for the workers; silver and gold threads; approximately 50 pairs of bobbins.

Technique: Cloth stitch; plaits; tow yarn; twists.

Size: Approximately 7 × 7½ in. (17 × 18 cm.).

Pattern: Paper sketch.

Procedure: Make the lace on a rotating porous square so that you get a good general view of the work. Spool the pairs together two by two in order to begin with a closed braid. Put up the passives, alternating coarse and thin threads. Start the cloth stitches from the left. In the entire work there will be about ten workers, all of which carry yarn of the same coarseness. The drawing, fig. 3–4, indicates by the sign ∩ where to insert the new pairs. New pairs are introduced and removed continually, as shown in the drawing and the photograph, figs. 3–4 and 6. The plaits are made with either two or three pairs. (Plaits made with three pairs are marked with an A in the drawing.) Place the pins as regularly as possible in the braid; in the rest of the lace the location of the pins depends upon the appearance of work itself. Weave away the thinner threads when finishing-off the lace.

Fig. 3–5. Detail of a plait with three pairs, marked A in the drawing.

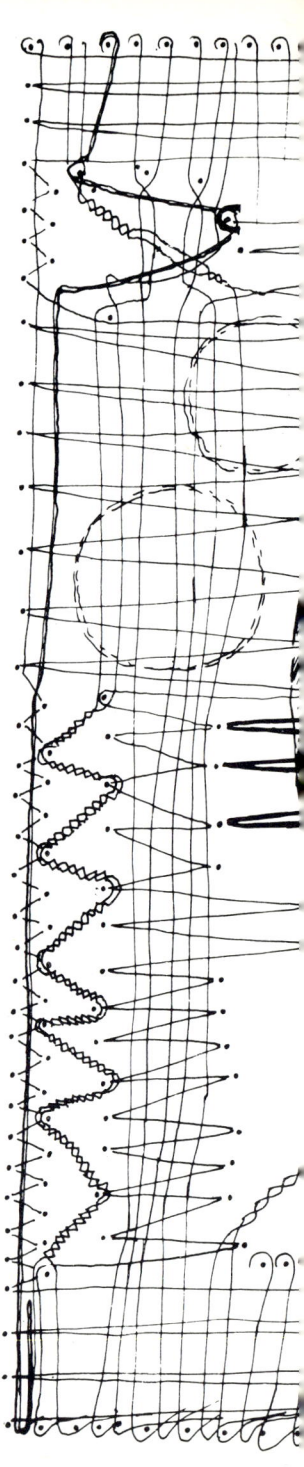

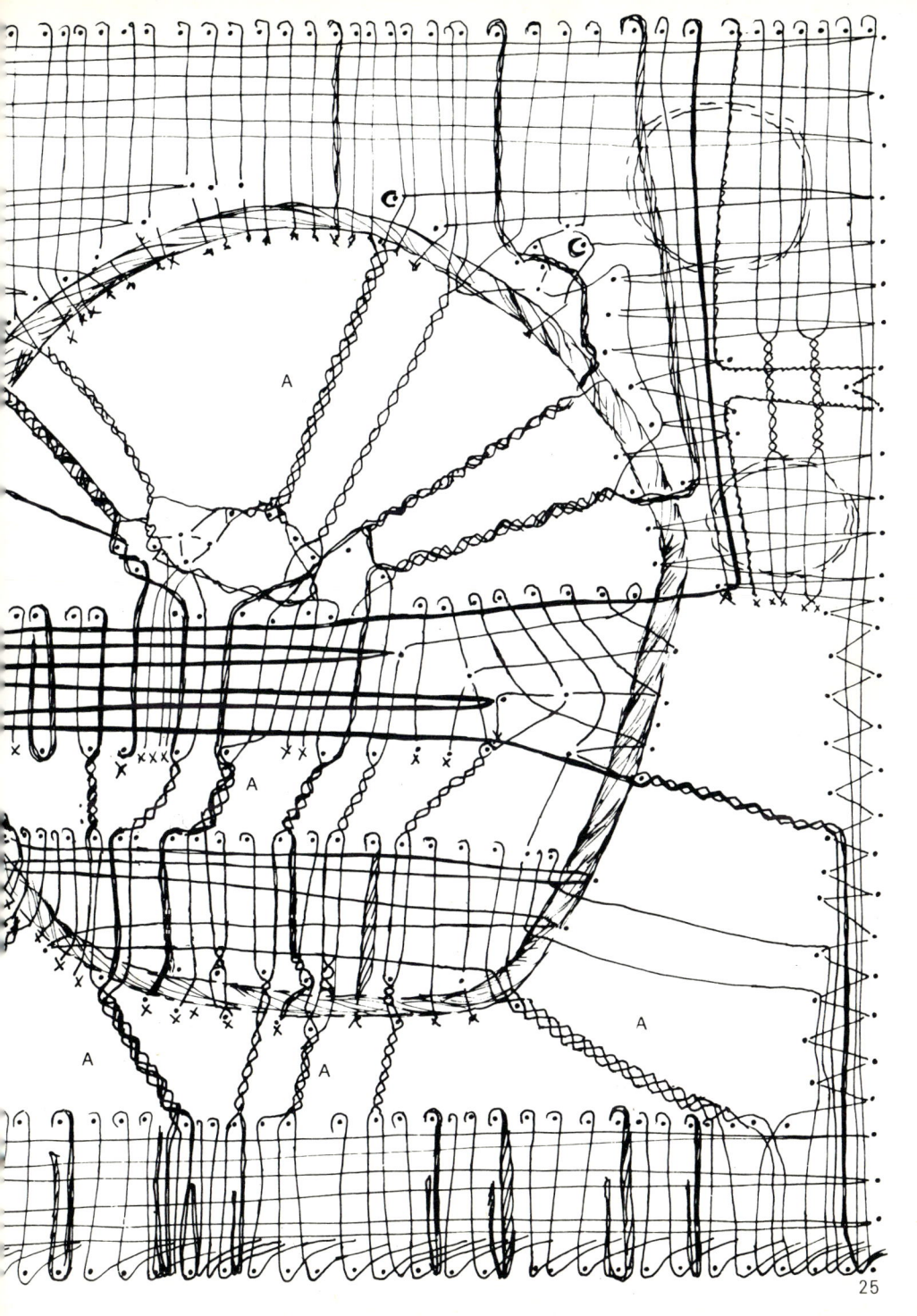

Fig. 3–6. Modus vivendi, designed by Mariann Lövgren and executed by Hildur Kratz.

Cut off the coarser threads. Thread the silver and gold rings into the lace with a needle.

Fitting: Attach the lace in the two upper corners as invisibly as possible, with thin nylon thread.

Red picture

This is an experimental decorative lace.

Material: Linen yarn no. 16/2; linen tow; Finnish linen yarn (all in reddish tones).
Technique: Torchon ground.
Pattern: Paper sketch pinned onto a hardboard square.
Procedure: There is no set method for this lace; the pairs of bobbins are brought in and removed according to the free pattern.

Only the ground is determined in advance. The lace is finished-off with a fringe in which the threads are tied together in pairs.
Fitting: The lace is attached to firm cotton fabric in three colours (yellow, red, and orange).

Fig. 3–7. Red picture (detail), designed and executed by Mariann Lövgren. See colour plate 6, opposite p. 33.

Portrait

Material: Coloured linen yarn no. 16/2; contouring thread; coloured Finnish linen yarn.

Technique: Cloth stitch; net, double cloth stitch, and torchon grounds; plaits; cords.

Size: 2½ × 4 in. (6 × 9·6 cm.).

Pattern: Paper sketch.

Procedure: Make the lace on a porous plate or a pillow. Weave the upper frame, then bring in extra pairs for the head. The face is made straight across from one side to the other, twisting round the coloured threads. Make the cords on the sides with pairs from either the face or the frame. Insert and remove new pairs as you need them.

Fitting: A piece of linen about 1 in. (2·4 cm.) larger than the lace on all sides is required for fitting the lace. Make a hanger from a piece of metal thread.

Fasten the threads on the back of the picture, and knot those from the lower part of the frame. Stretch the work under a damp cloth. Pull out a thread from each side of the piece of linen so that the inner measures correspond to the size of the lace, and hem stitch round the linen. Thread the yarns from the lower frame through the seam and fasten them in the hem. Stitch the other three sides into the seam. Stretch the entire article again under a damp cloth. Pass the metal thread through the upper hem, and twist the ends together.

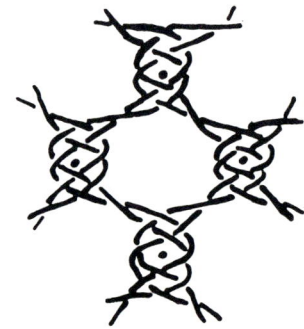

Fig. 3–8. Pattern drawing in full scale.

Fig. 3–9. Detail of the ground stitch in the left cheek.

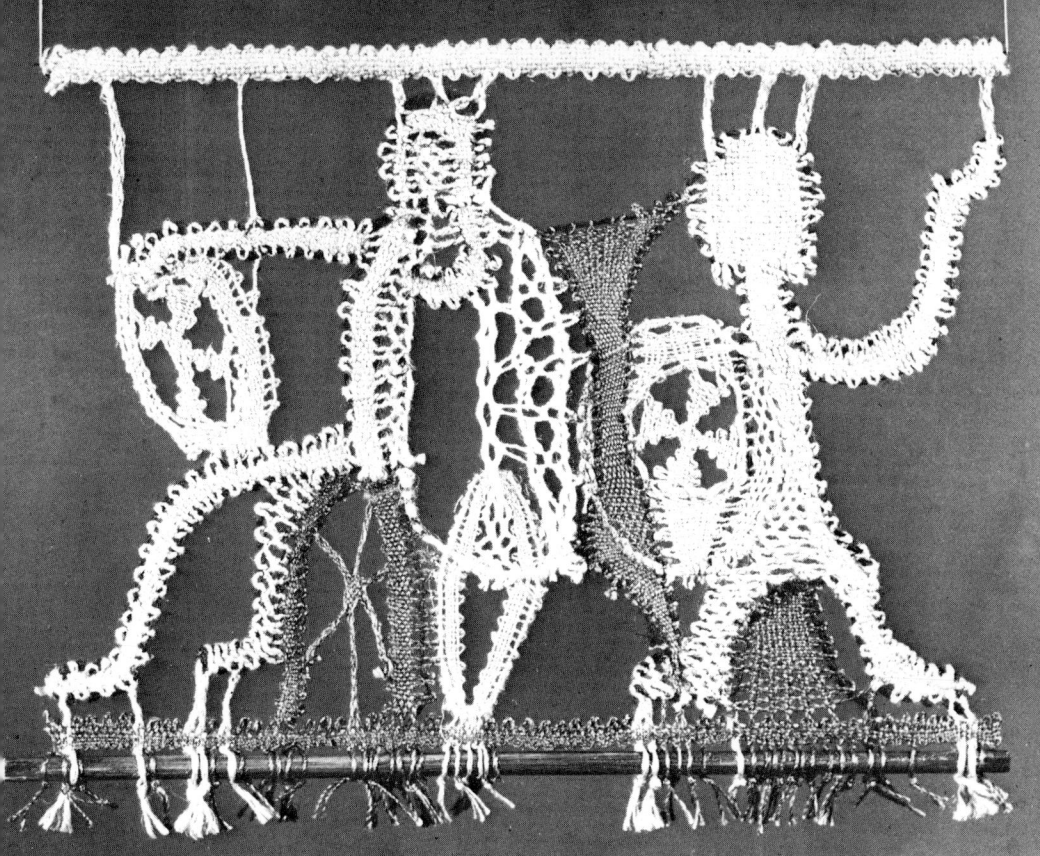

*Fig. 3–10. Fredrik and Valfrid, designed and
executed by Mariann Lövgren.*

Fredrik and Valfrid

Material: Bleached and coloured linen
yarn no. 16/2; unbleached thread no. 8/2
for contouring; tow yarn no. 6; Finnish
linen yarn.
Technique: Cloth stitch, torchon and net
grounds; plaits; cords.
Size: 9½ × 7 in. (23 × 17 cm.).
Pattern: Paper sketch.
Procedure: Use a porous square since the
bobbins move in so many different
directions. Make the cloth stitch ground as
simply as possible — for example, in the
direction of the upper braid. Use the pairs
from the figures as weft threads in the
lower braid, bringing in extra pairs as
needed. Finish-off with pearl knots. Add

the contouring threads, and twist the pairs
round them.

In figures (like Valfrid's head) where
cloth stitch and net grounds are in the
same colours, work horizontally, making
cloth stitches and half-stitches straight
across the figure.

Retain the yarn ends from pairs that are
removed during the work, and fasten them
after you have finished the lace. Insert new
pairs in existing grounds with a crocheting
needle, and tie them to a thread or pin them
up when you start working with them.
Routine: Complete the different sections of
the lace in the following order: upper braid,
Fredrik's arm and head, the brown ground,
and the shield parallel with the body;

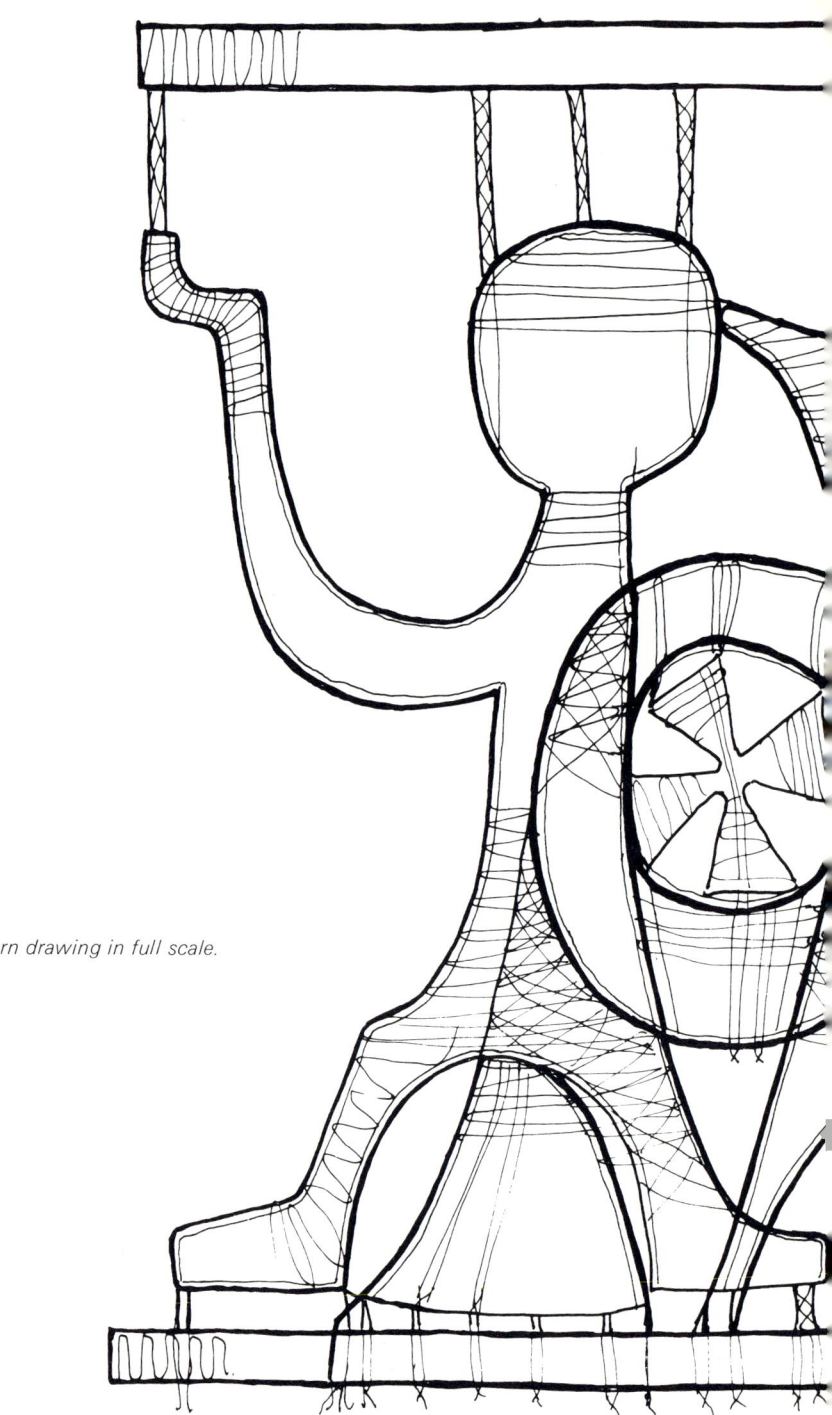

Fig. 3–11. Pattern drawing in full scale.

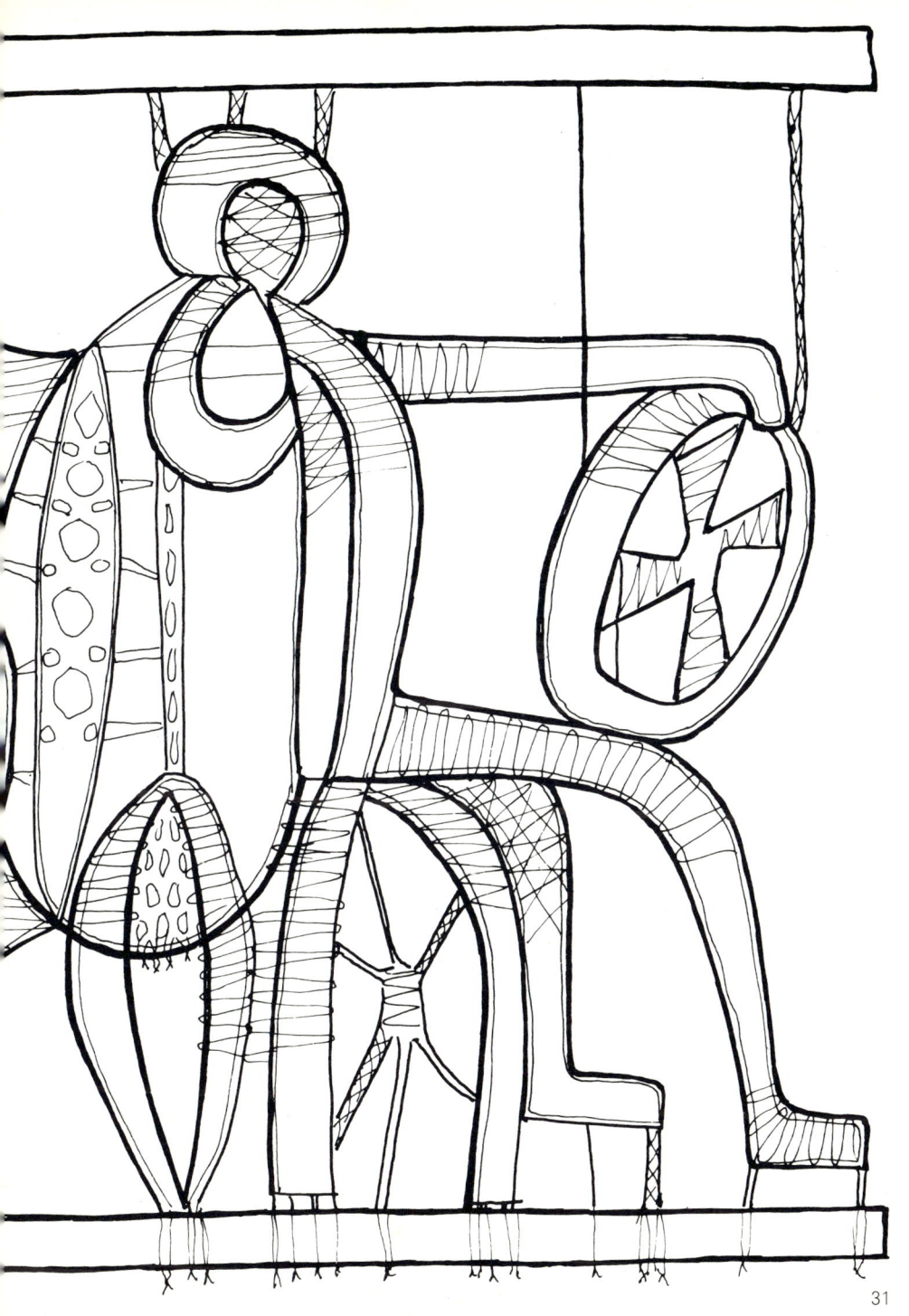

Valfrid figure, and the white and orange circular grounds; Valfrid's shield (fasten it to his knee afterwards); the orange and brown grounds; the spider; the lower braid.

Fitting: For the fitting you need two sticks of the same length as the braids. Paint one of the sticks brown to match the lower braid. Then fasten the threads at the back of the lace, and stretch the finished lace between damp cloths. Fix the brown stick in the lower braid with pearl knots, cutting an even fringe. Stitch the other stick onto the back of the upper braid.

Colour plate 1. Portrait, designed and executed by Mariann Lövgren. This lace is described on p. 27.

Colour plate 2. Mother Sweden, designed and executed by Elisabeth Hallberg. This lace is made from wool, strings, silver threads, and wooden beads, using only cloth stitches.

Colour plate 3. Field of flowers, designed and executed by Birgitta Eriksson. Materials for this lace are rayon yarn, Finnish linen yarn, and hemp strings in various shades of blue and green. The lace is made with cloth stitches and plaits.

Entrance

This lace is designed to attract your attention, yet it is very simple to make. The pattern consists of only two stitches: cloth stitch and double cloth stitch, which correspond to the firm material. The lace is fixed between two sticks of juniper wood. The yarns are threaded in pairs through small holes in the sticks, and the ends are tied with ordinary knots. A skilled person needs only three hours to complete this lace.

Material: Unbleached linen yarn no. 8/2; 8 pairs of bobbins; 2 wooden sticks 6 in. (15 cm.) long.

Technique: Cloth stitch; double cloth stitch.

Size: The lace itself is about 2 in. (4·8 cm.) wide. The entire window decoration is about $6 \times 7\frac{1}{4}$ in. (14 × 17 cm.).

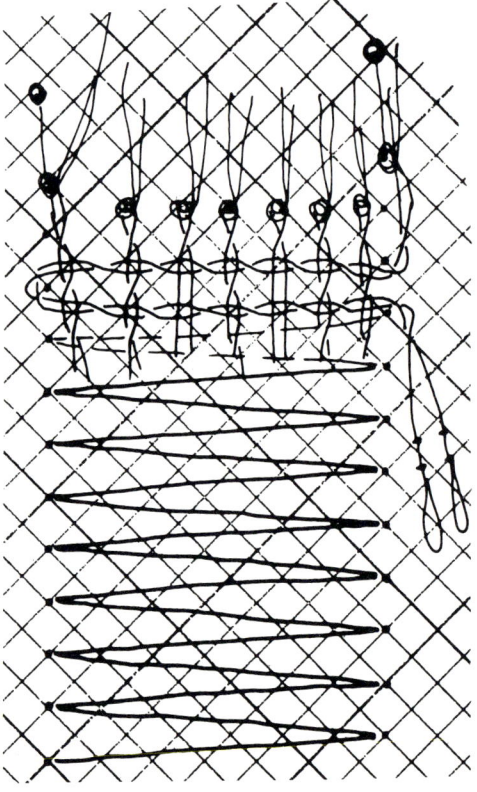

Fig. 3–12. Pattern drawing.

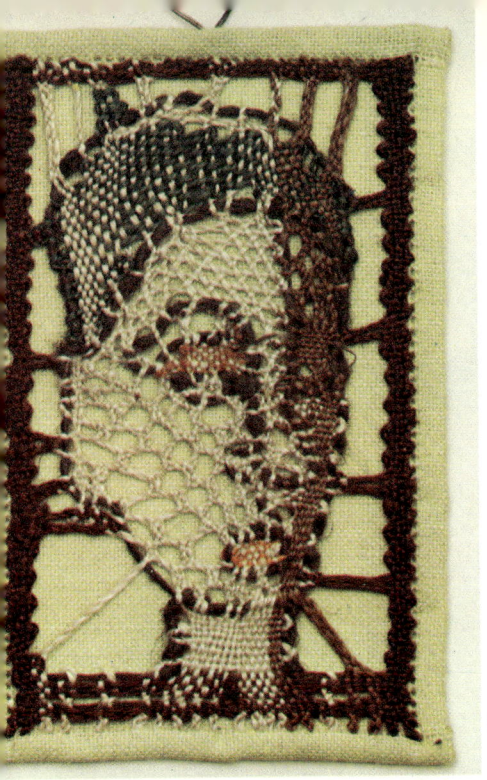

1.

2.

our plate 4. Norbotten, designed and
cuted by Monica Wikberg. This lace is
de of black wool ends fitted on green jute,
it is done entirely with cloth stitches.

Colour plate 5. City by the water, designed and
executed by Birgitta Rudeskog. The materials
for this lace are fishing line, wool, and velvet
ribbon.

4.

5.

Fig. 3–13. Fasten the
pairs with a crochet loop
that you can dissolve.

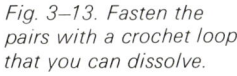

Colour plate 6. Red picture. This lace is
described on p. 27.

Fig. 3–14. Entrance, designed and executed by
Anna Karin Johansson.

Pattern: Drawing in full scale on $\frac{1}{4}$ in.
(6 mm.) square-ruled paper.

Procedure: Put up the sticks as shown in
the drawing, fig. 3–12. Fasten the pairs
with a crochet loop, as in the detailed
sketch, fig. 3–13. Begin with an ordinary
cloth stitch ground, but give an extra twist
to the workers when turning. The drawing
shows the direction of the workers. Make
one row of double cloth stitches between
the cloth stitch grounds. Construct a
second ground of double cloth stitch, cloth
stitch, double cloth stitch, cloth stitch,
etc., making double cloth stitch, twist, pin,
and double cloth stitch when turning. The
lace starts and finishes with this ground.
Each piece of lace should be 6 in. (14 cm.)
long. Make sure that the threads are about
4 in. (9·6 cm.) long at both ends.

Fig. 3–15. This lace fits into many surroundings. Here it serves as a window screen.

Fitting: Drill 16 holes in each of the sticks. Thread the yarns two by two through the holes with a needle, and knot them. Hang the lace in a window frame with two nylon lines through the end holes of the upper stick.

Pond in the woods

This lace shows how well wood and textiles harmonize. The mirror is made from old pine wood and the lace from coarse green-brown linen yarn.

Material: Coloured linen yarn no. 8/2 or 16/2 doubled; 4 pairs of bobbins.

Technique: Cloth stitch.

Size: The pattern is 5 in. (12 cm.) in diameter. The mirror is 6 in. (14 cm.) in diameter, and the handle is $6\frac{1}{4}$ in. (15 cm.) long.

Pattern: Paper sketch.

Procedure: The lace should be made on a revolving pillow or plate since the work proceeds successively from beginning to end. You can either work freely or follow the wedge pattern in the sketch, fig. 3–17 on page 94. Put in the pins round the circumference far enough away from each other and askew from the edges so that you can stretch the cloth stitches sufficiently. (See the section on separate pins in Chapter 9.) Place the pins increasingly closer to each other as you approach the inner edge. Stretch the passives in the same direction as the circular pattern.

Fitting: Stitch the lace as invisibly as possible onto a piece of linen that suits it in colour and coarseness. Sew the beads on

Fig. 3–16. Pond in the woods, designed and executed by Kristina Malmberg. This lace is fitted on a suitably coarse piece of linen in the right colour. The beads are sewn on afterwards.

afterwards. Fold in the linen so that it does not protrude beyond the lace, and tack or press carefully to keep it in place. If you want a sturdier support glue the lace onto a piece of pasteboard or felt the same size as the motif. Finally, glue the finished articles to the back of the mirror.

4. Festivals

This chapter is especially for children. The designs are stimulating, yet simple enough for classes in schools.

Collection bag

A coarse lace like Fields with squares is most suitable for this article. The pattern for this design is provided in fig. 8–26.

Size: The complete bag, including the handle, is 28 in. (70 cm.) long. It is 4¾ in. (1·4 cm.) high without the hangers, and its diameter is 5¼ in. (12·6 cm.).

Material: Bag holder; 8 complete sections of the pattern; 2⅕ yd. (2 m.) linen or corded ribbon ¾ in. (1·8 cm.) wide in the

Fig. 4–1. Collection bag, designed and executed by Ingegärd Kärvedahl.

same colour as the bag: 15 × 6 in. (40 × 14 cm.) thin linen fabric or leather for the lining.

Procedure: Machine-sew the pattern sections together two by two. Hem the squares straight across the top, but join them in a tip at the bottom. Cast-on the sides together. Cut out the lining according to the pattern, fig. 4–2. If you are using linen make sure to allow enough for the seam. A leather lining is zig-zagged together edge to edge on the machine. Turn the bag inside-out, steam-press on a paper or wood form, and let it dry overnight. Cut eight strips of ribbon 4 in. (9·6 cm.) long to fasten the bag to the holder, and cast them on firmly. Edge both the inside and the outside of the bag with ribbon. (You will need 16 in. (40 cm.) of ribbon $\frac{3}{4}$ in. (1·8 cm.) wide.) For the tassel,

Fig. 4–2. Part of the pattern.

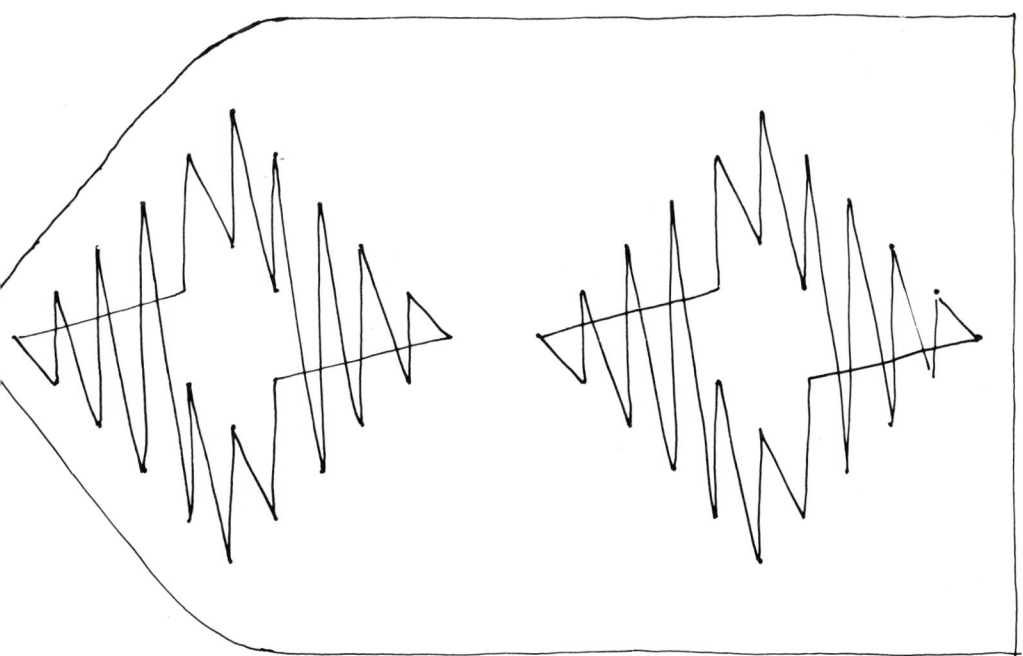

Fig. 4–3. The collection bag in full length

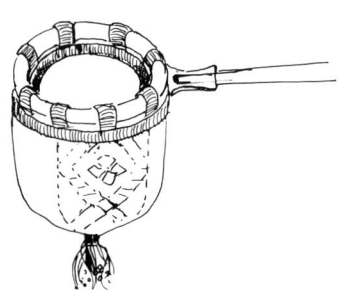

Fig. 4–4. The collection bag from above,
showing how to fit the linen ribbons.

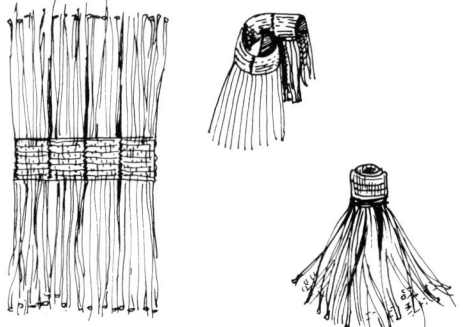

Fig. 4–5. How to make the tassel.

cut four ribbons 4 in. (9·6 cm.) long, and
fray them until $\frac{3}{4}$ in. (1·8 cm.) is left in the
middle. Sew them together, fold them in
the centre, roll them into a hard ball, and
fasten the ends firmly. The size of the tassel
will depend on how many ribbons you
join together.

Fig. 4–6. Christening robe, designed by
Birgitta Werner-Johansson and Naime Thorlin
and executed by Daga Zamul.

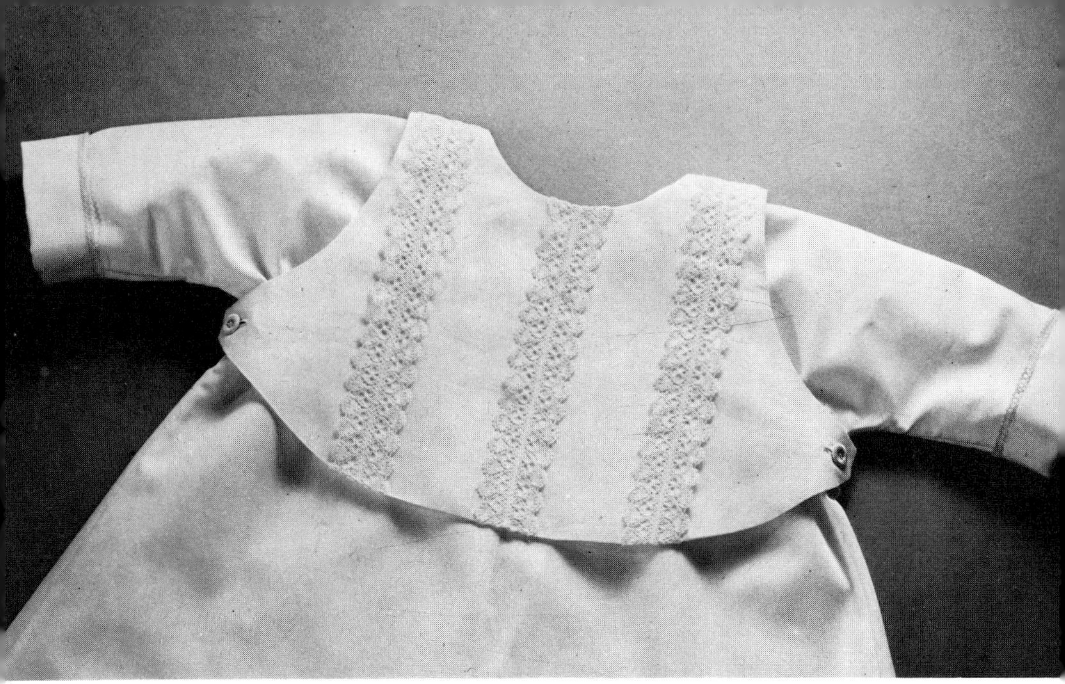

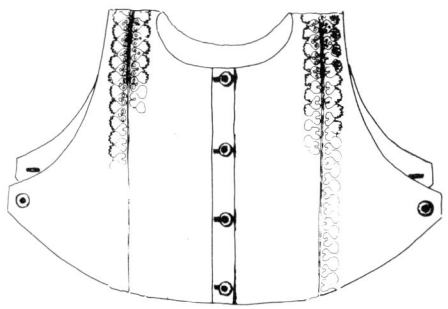

Fig. 4–7. A yoke for the christening robe.

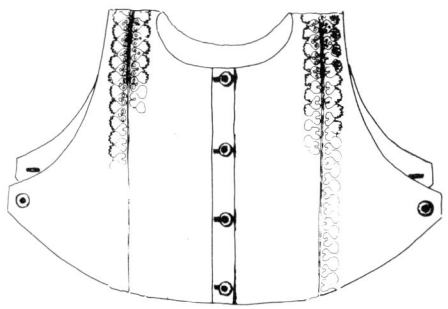

Fig. 4–8. Detail of the back of the yoke.

Christening robe

Material: Cotton for the dress; Irish linen for the yoke; linen thread no. 80/2.

Technique: Cloth stitch; picot; braid.

Pattern: Reversed hearts for the yoke; picot and braid for the edgings.

Procedure: The robe is made in two parts, the dress itself in cotton and the yoke in linen, which is decorated with lace and thread buttons. You may vary the amount of lace from a couple of rows to the entire yoke, and you can use any thin pattern. The dress is entirely machine-sewn except for the lace itself. The hem, the back split, and the cuffs are also trimmed with lace.

5. Lampshades and lights

There are many ways to combine light and lace. Completely new light effects can be achieved by making small alterations in old patterns or by using coloured yarns.

Gallery bracket lamp

This is an advanced lace, composed of a variety of grounds and stitches. You can use sections of it in other designs.

Material: Semi-bleached linen yarn no. 40/2; 66 pairs of bobbins; 6 extra pairs of bobbins to bring in as the work proceeds.

Technique: Cloth stitch; net, double cloth stitch, and torchon grounds; twists.

Size: 6 × 8 in. (14 × 20 cm.).

Procedure: The drawing in full scale, fig. 5–2, shows the method. Irregularities are explained in detail; the simpler parts are more schematic.

Spool the bobbins together two by two, and put up the pins as shown in the drawing. Start the lace with two rows of double cloth stitch without pins. Two pairs follow each other from left to right, giving the first and upper pair an extra twist.

Stick pins in the corners as shown in the drawing. The corners on both sides will look the same. The main ground in the motif is a torchon ground with twists, but it alters with the trees to cloth stitch and net grounds. Bring in the extra pairs where the sign ∩ appears, and remove four of them where marked by the sign ✕. The other extra pairs remain throughout the work.

The lace becomes irregular with the house. The loose parts round the roof require extra twists and some double cloth stitches without pins. Inside the roof (the gallery) the passives are twisted approximately twelve times, depending on how firmly you

work the lace. Stretch the pairs in the cloth stitch ground on the roof carefully.

The net grounds round the trees are regular except for one square just to the right of the roof where the workers go right instead of left. The house structure is completely in double cloth stitch without pins. Stretch the pairs carefully and regularly. Note that you make a double cloth stitch

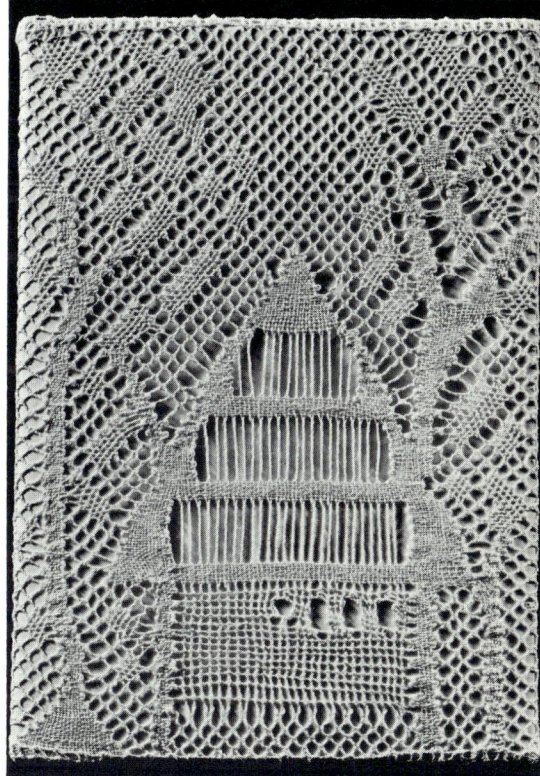

Fig. 5–1. Gallery bracket lamp, designed and executed by Gertrude Ström.

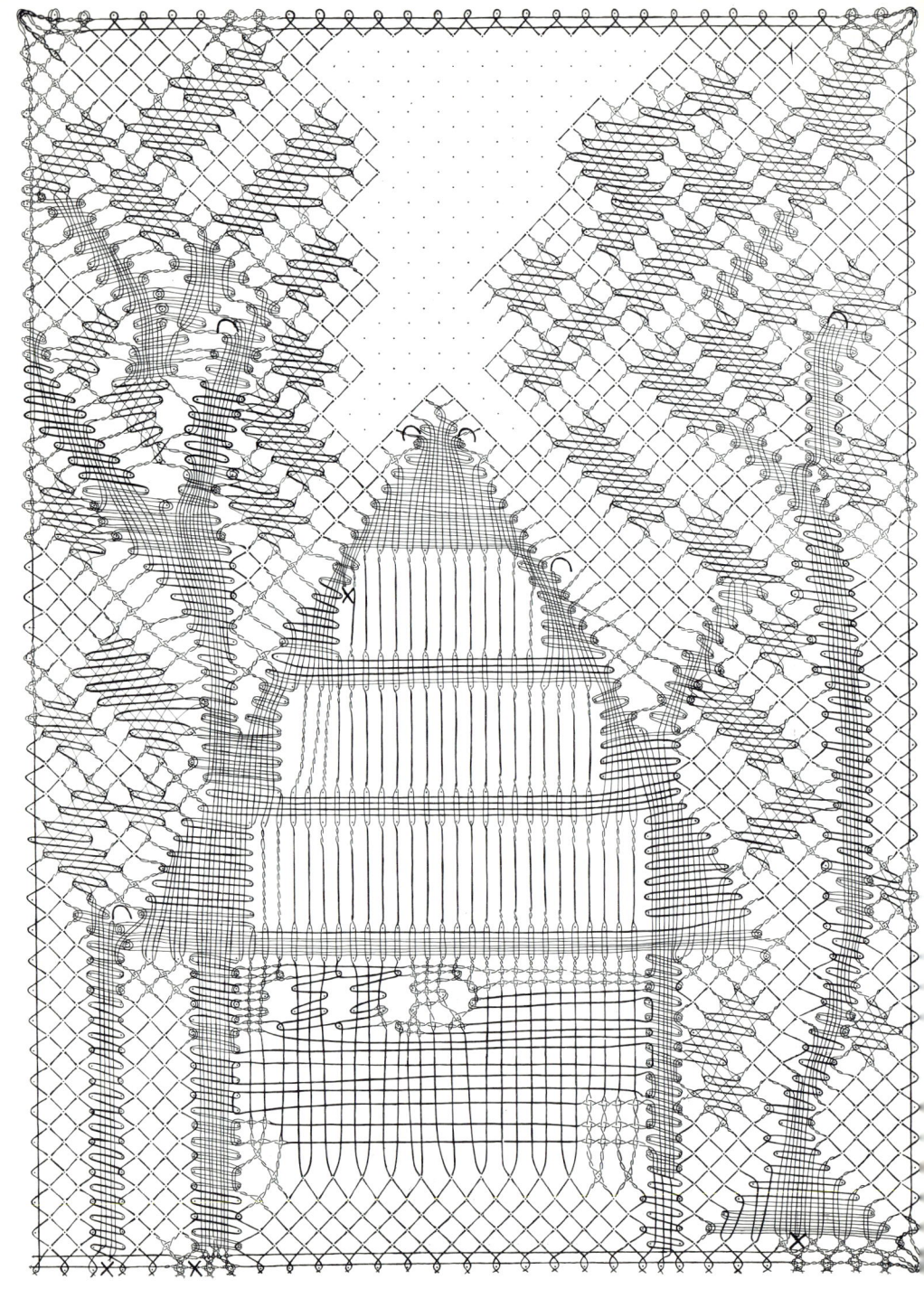

42

Fig. 5—2. Work drawing for the Gallery bracket lamp

without a pin in the right-hand corner of the ground. Continue the lace as indicated in the drawing.

Finish the lace as you started it, with two rows of double cloth stitches, but this time give the lower pair an extra twist. Make another row of double cloth stitch, then tie the pairs away one by one from left to right. Thread the last pair on the right back into the lace with a needle. You can also finish-off the lace by tying away the pairs with cloth stitches, which results in a closed braid. (See the section on finishing-off in Chapter 9.)

Fitting: Fold the end threads over to the back of the lace when fixing it on a lamp.

Shoemaker's lamp

The shoemaker's lamp popular at the turn of the century inspired this modern variation decorated with lace and beads. The lamp is made of semi-crystal and blown in a graphite mould. Both the upper and the lower ends are polished. Through the combination of glass, thin wool, and gold-coloured glass beads the light glows beautifully.

Material: 12 × 12 in. (29 × 29 cm.) white hand-woven worsted wool yarn; 10 in. (25 cm.) white cotton or lace ribbon $\frac{1}{4}$ in. (6 mm.) wide for edging.

Size: The finished shade (without the lace) measures 11 in. (26·4 cm.) in diameter at the bottom and 3 in. (7·2 cm.) at the top. Its circumference is 38 in. (92 cm.), and it is $4\frac{1}{2}$ in. (10·8 cm.) high.

Technique: Plaits.

Pattern: Bead fringe. (See 'Bead fringe for curtains' in Chapter 2 for the necessary information.)

Procedure: Make a circular paper pattern in the given measurements with a pair of compasses or a pencil on a string $5\frac{1}{2}$ in. (13 cm.) long, fastening the string with a drawing pin to the middle of the paper. Cut the circle out of the fabric, allowing for a hem $\frac{1}{4}$ in. (6 mm.) wide at the bottom and

Fig. 5–3. Shoemaker's lamp decorated with lace edging.

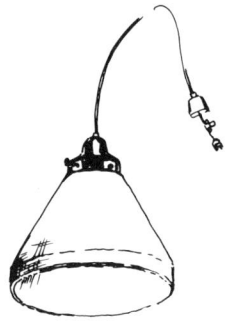

Fig. 5–5. The lamp without the textile shade.

Fig. 5–4. Shoemaker's lamp decorated with bead fringe, designed by Amie Stalkrantz and Naime Thorlin and executed by Anna Rynestad.

the top. Zig-zag all the edges on a machine. Stitch the ribbon onto the top edge, then fold up both the fabric and the ribbon. (This folding will be hidden by the brass socket.) Fold in and sew the bottom hem. The lace should be joined together beforehand and should be slightly wider than the shade. Pin the lace onto the outer side of the shade, stitch it, fold it down, and press the seam carefully.

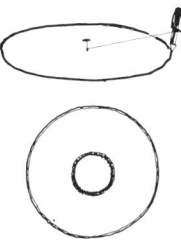

Fig. 5–6. Circular paper pattern made with a pencil on a string.

Peg lamp

A lamp suspended above a table creates a cosy and friendly atmosphere. This lamp is so simply constructed that you can put it together yourself. The turned pine pieces have eight round holes where wooden pegs of nearly the same dimension are fitted. The pegs have scores on top to hold the shade, which is fitted like a skirt round the construction.

Size: The wood construction is 12 in. (28·8 cm.) high. The wooden socket is $2\frac{3}{4}$ in. (6·6 cm.) in diameter, and the pegs are each $6\frac{1}{2}$ in. (15·6 cm.) long. The lamp is 16 in. (38·4 cm.) in diameter. There is an inner shade to diminish the heat from the bulb, which measures 6 in. (14·4 cm.) in height and $3\frac{3}{4}$–$4\frac{1}{2}$ in. (9–11 cm.) in diameter. The finished shade is $9\frac{1}{4}$ in. (23 cm.) high and 68 in. (170 cm.) in circumference. The lace is $1\frac{1}{4}$ in. (3 cm.) wide, as is the gathering.

Procedure: The textile shade is made of worsted yarn cloth edged with the lace 'Playing brownies', which is described in Chapter 2. Naturally, other fabrics and laces can be used. Overcast the hems, and stitch on the lace, by hand. The gathering has a canal for an elastic band.

Fig. 5–8. Peg lamp, designed and executed by John Wulff and Naime Thorlin.

Fig. 5–7. How to construct the lamp.

Tube

The lace is made on a cylindrical lamp-shade. This method has the advantage that there will be no seams on the lace. You can make the shade from a square piece of lace, but you will have an ugly seam.

Material: Strips of coarse white cotton (such as sheet fabric); hemp string.

Technique: Double cloth stitches.

Size: The finished shade measures $9\frac{1}{2}$ in. (23 cm.) in height, 7 in. (17 cm.) in diameter, and $22\frac{1}{2}$ in. (56 cm.) in circumference. The lace is $\frac{1}{4}$ in. (6 mm.) longer than the shade so that the ends can be folded round the edges.

Pattern: The lace is made on a round shade covered with a pricking card, three layers of felt, and chequered fabric with $\frac{3}{4}$ in. (1·8 cm.) squares that serves as the pattern.

Procedure: Cut the cotton fabric in strips $\frac{1}{2}$ in. (1·2 cm.) wide. Throughout the work each cotton strip is used together with a piece of string. Estimate the length of the strips to four times the height of the shade. There is no need to roll them up; they can hang loose. Fasten the pricking card round the frame with glass-fibre tape, then wind the felt three times round it, and fix with textile glue. Fit the chequered fabric on in the same manner. Place the shade on a small table, and work your way round it.

You will need 56 pairs of strips and strings. Fasten them two by two with pins round the roll. Make a double cloth stitch, and place the pins as in 'Striped curtains' in Chapter 2. (See the drawing, fig. 5–9.)

When the work is finished take the lace off the roll, but leave the pins holding the last row of double cloth stitches together. Cut off the strings and one of the strips adjoining each pin, keeping the other strip to fold over the ends and stitch them to the back.

Fitting: You will need a lamp frame, lining, and stretchy white cotton ribbons twice as long as the circumference.

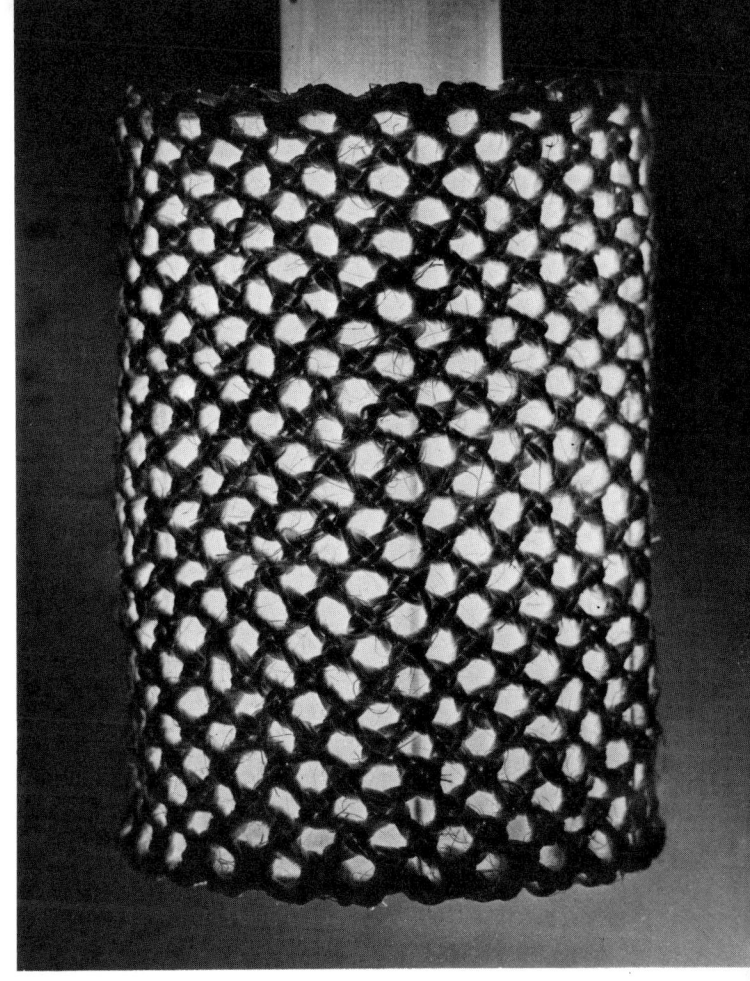

Fig. 5—9. How to hang the
strips on the standing reel.

Fig. 5—10. Tube, designed and executed by
Ingegerd Gyrulf.

Cover the frame in vellum paper or thin
poplin, otherwise the light will be too
bright. Cast-on the ribbons at the top and
bottom. Fold the lining round the frame
(leaving the paper loose) and stitch it and
the vellum to the ribbon at both ends. Put
the round lace-work over the frame. Fold
the ends round the upper and lower rings,
and stitch them to the cotton ribbon.

Turner's joy

Lamps and lace can be combined in many ways. This is a table lamp with a base made of turned pine and a narrow cylindrical shade decorated with lace round the top. A base or a shade can be made to order to match the measurements of a given lace.

Size: The entire lamp is $15\frac{1}{4}$ in. (36·6 cm.) high. The turned foot measures $6\frac{1}{2}$ in. (15·6 cm.) in height and 4 in. (9·6 cm.) in diameter. The shade is 10 in. (24 cm.) high and $3\frac{3}{4}$ in. (9 cm.) in diameter. The lace is $1\frac{3}{4}$ in. (4·2 cm.) wide.

Fig. 5–11. A plain lampshade like Turner's joy must be fitted expertly: Wind cotton ribbons round the top and bottom of the cylinder. The vellum lining is loose round the frame. Sew the textile lampshade together separately, and cover the lining with it. Stitch it to the cotton ribbons. Finally, stitch the lace invisibly to the shade.

Lapland huts

Material: Blue or orange yarn; 8 pairs of bobbins; green or yellow yarn; 18 pairs of bobbins.
Technique: Cloth stitch; rose ground; double cloth stitch.
Size: 2 in. (4·8 cm.) wide; one complete section of the pattern is 2½ in. (6 cm.) long.

Fig. 5–12. Lapland huts, designed and executed by Ulla Fagerlin, is a lace with points on both sides and an interesting colour scheme. The rose ground is in a single colour. You can also use bleached and unbleached lace yarn no. 35 instead of coloured threads.

Fig. 5–13. A beautiful lace can be used in many ways.

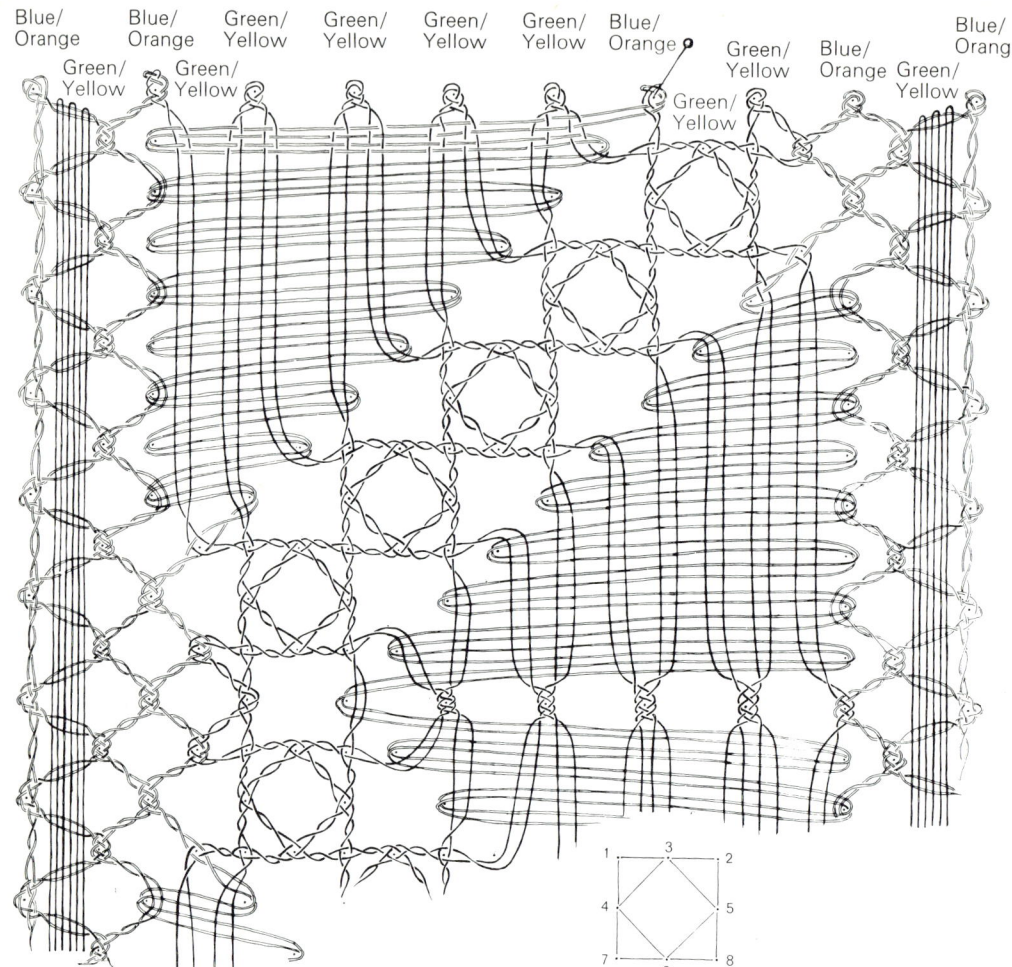

Blue/ Blue/ Green/ Green/ Green/ Green/ Blue/ Green/ Blue/ Blue/
Orange Orange Yellow Yellow Yellow Yellow Orange Yellow Orange Orange
Green/ Green/ Green/ Green/
Yellow Yellow Yellow Yellow

1 3 2
4   5
7 6 8

Fig. 5–14. Work drawing.

Fig. 5–15. Schematic sketch showing the order of the stitches in the rose ground.

Procedure: Spool the bobbins together two by two. Put up the pairs with pins followed by double cloth stitches. At the point marked by the pin in the drawing, fig. 5–14, the workers pass immediately to the cloth stitch ground with a cloth stitch. Be careful with the order of the colours: in the drawing blue or orange yarns are marked with double lines.

Make the picot with double cloth stitches, giving an extra twist to the outer pair; the inner pair (the workers) passes through three pairs with cloth stitches. Twist the workers once before joining them to the pairs in the double cloth stitch ground. Both sides have the same construction. Make the entire cloth stitch ground parallel with the picot, as shown in

Fig. 5–16. Lapland huts fitted on a candle glass that is blown in a mould and cut by hand. This example of the lace was designed and executed by Amie Stalkrantz and Naime Thorlin.

the drawing. Twist the green (or yellow) passives once.

Start the rose ground with half-stitch, pin, half-stitch, extra twist. Put up the pin as shown in the drawing. Note that the pairs from the rose ground do not take an extra twist.

Continue the cloth stitch ground and the picot on the right-hand side.

When the lace is long enough to go round the candle glass finish it off with three rows of cloth stitch ground so that it corresponds to the beginning. Tie the pairs together with reef knots, as shown in fig. 7–11. To join the ends together, follow the description in the section on finishing-off in Chapter 9.

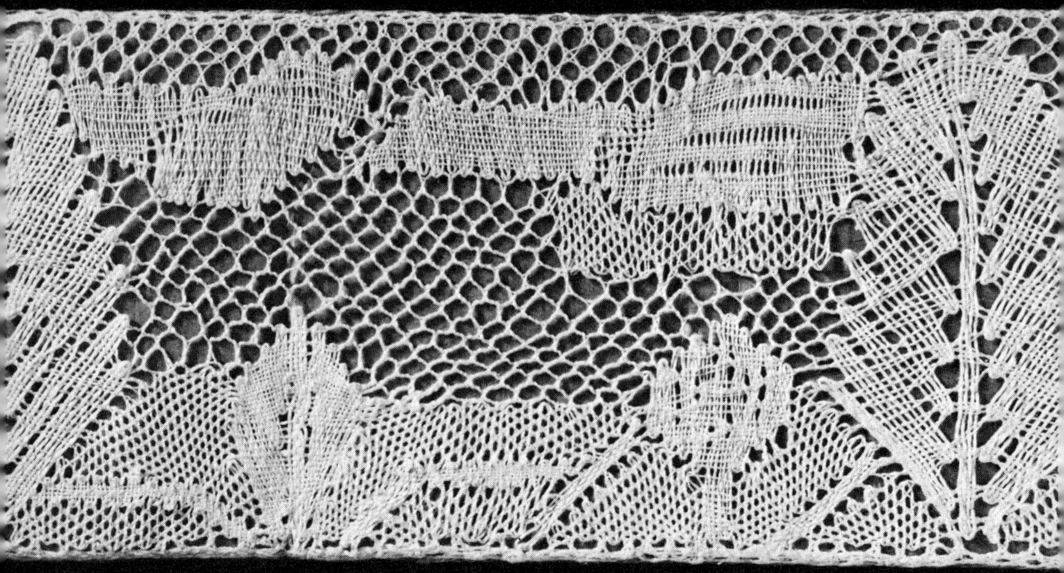

Fig. 5–17. Lake scene, designed and executed
by Gina Modin.

Fig. 5–18. House, designed and executed by
Ebba Eklund.

6. For table and window-seat

This chapter offers variations on traditional lace patterns for table-cloths and place-mats.

Swimming birds

The lace contains many basic grounds and stitches and is therefore an excellent lace for courses. The pattern is repeated regularly, but with enough variety to be an interesting practice lace.

Material: Unbleached linen yarn no. 60/2: 27 pairs of bobbins: weft yarn no. 18/2: 1 pair of bobbins: a $5\frac{1}{4}$ × $5\frac{1}{4}$ in. (12·6 × 12·6 cm.) piece of linen (35 threads/in., 14 threads/cm.).

Technique: Torchon ground with twists: net ground: cloth stitch: tallies: gimp: double cloth stitch without pins in the cloth stitch grounds.

Size: The lace is $1\frac{3}{4}$ in. (4·2 cm.) wide: one complete section of the pattern is 3 in. (7·2 cm.) long. The finished table-mat with lace is $8\frac{1}{4}$ × $8\frac{1}{4}$ in. (20 × 20 cm.).

Procedure: Spool the bobbins together two by two, and put up the pairs as shown in the drawing, fig. 6–3. Start with the picot: make a double cloth stitch and then cloth stitches through three pairs, twisting the workers. Bring in a new pair at the next pin: make a half-stitch, lift the pin, push up the stitch, and replace the pin in the same hole. Make another half-stitch, and give an extra twist to the left pair: the right pair goes into the cloth stitch ground without an extra twist. Return through three pairs in the cloth stitch ground. Twist the workers once, then make double cloth stitch, extra twist, pin, and double cloth stitch in the picot, as in the drawing. Bring in new pairs for the torchon ground with twists. Put in the gimp with only one twist before and after. Note that the two threads cross where the net ground starts. The net ground is done with half-stitch up to the tallies, which are explained in the section on tallies in Chapter 9.

Continue the torchon ground with twists and weft inlays to the bird's tail, which consists of cloth stitch ground with two different kinds of loose edges. For the broad edge, join the passives two by two, twist them, half-stitch, pin, and half-stitch. For the narrow edge, twist the workers once and twice. Follow the drawing in every detail.

![Swimming birds lace place-mat]

Fig. 6—1. Swimming birds, designed by Ulla
Fagerlin and executed by Margareta Svensson.

Fig. 6—2. This lace can be
fitted on a window frame.

The braid is made in the usual way:
Double cloth stitch, double cloth stitch,
extra twist, pin, and double cloth stitch.
Continue making the bird with cloth
stitches and weft inlays. One of the pairs of
passives changes place with the workers in
the cloth stitch ground to form the bird's
eye. Carry on with the net ground and the
tallies until the weft threads cross, then
make another bird facing the first one.
Follow the drawing to complete the entire
square. Finish-off the lace by repeating the
first row in the torchon ground, and tie the
threads two by two.

Fitting: Stitch the ends in the first and last
rows together as invisibly as possible on
the reverse side. Cast-off the knots on
the reverse side tightly.

The place-mat by itself is $4\frac{1}{2}$ × $4\frac{1}{2}$ in.
(10·8 × 10·8 cm.) when finished, and it has
a $\frac{1}{4}$ in. (6 mm.) hem. To make the mat, cut a
square $5\frac{1}{4}$ × $5\frac{1}{4}$ in. (12·6 × 12·6 cm.) from
the linen; then fold the hem, tack it, and
sew down the corners. Hem-stitch from
underneath over three threads in the linen
with lace thread no. 80/2. Press the place-
mat.

Pin the lace on the linen from underneath. The lace is about $\frac{1}{4}$ in. (6 mm.)
longer than the linen; gather this width
towards the linen and stitch the lace on
carefully.

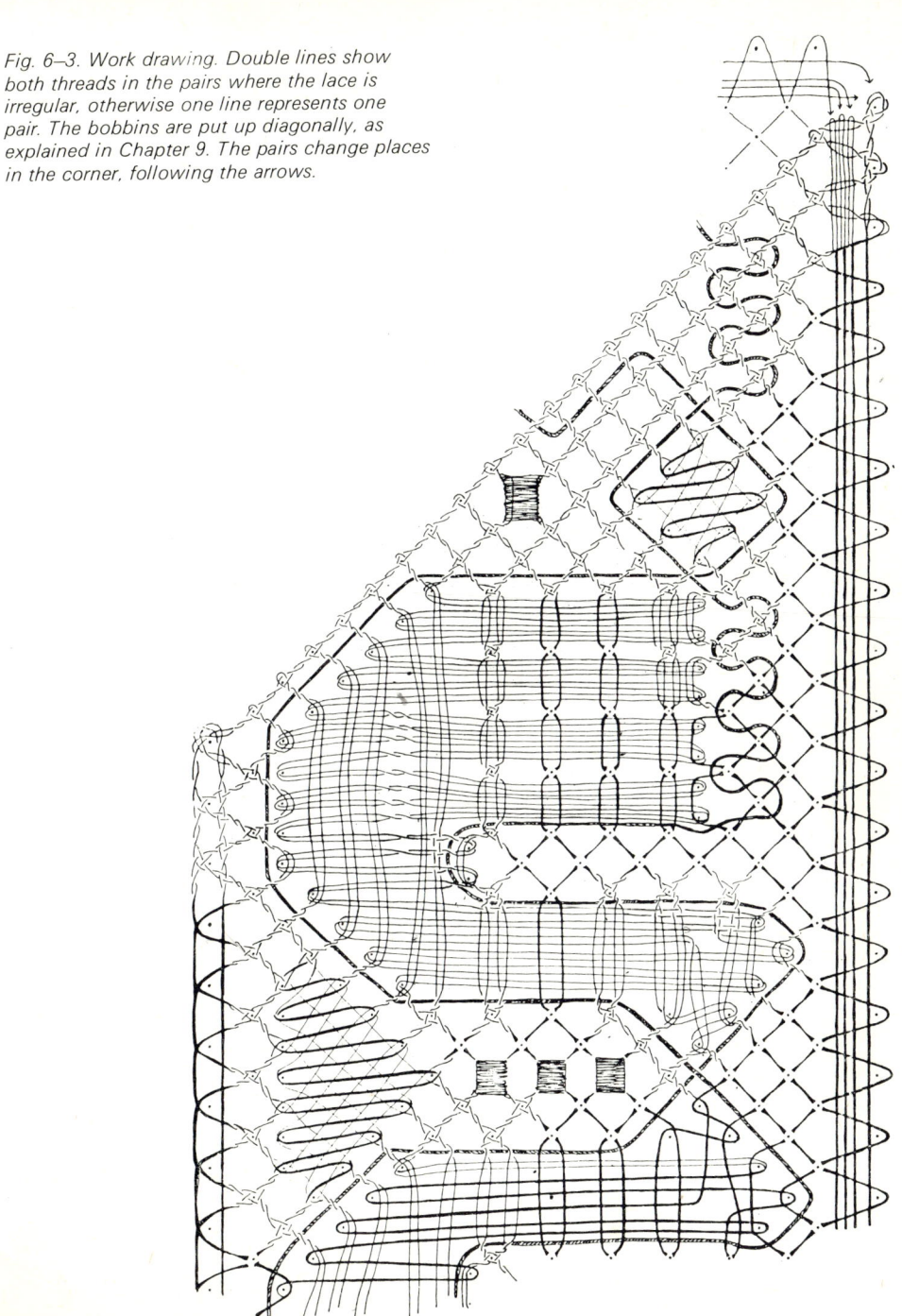

Fig. 6–3. Work drawing. Double lines show both threads in the pairs where the lace is irregular, otherwise one line represents one pair. The bobbins are put up diagonally, as explained in Chapter 9. The pairs change places in the corner, following the arrows.

Karin

This lace is made in weaving linen, which is soft to work with and stretches easily. It is therefore suitable for a lace with many cloth stitch grounds. The colours correspond to bleached and unbleached: 'unbleached' is dyed, and both are washable. Naturally, you can choose other colours, but they should not be too different.

Material: White weaving linen no. 16/2: 12 pairs of bobbins: beige weaving linen no. 16/2: 12 pairs of bobbins.

Technique: Cloth stitch and brabant grounds: spider: braid with open edge: loose edges in the cloth stitch ground.

Size: The lace is 2 in. (4·8 cm.) wide. One complete section of the pattern is $1\frac{3}{4}$ in. (4·2 cm.) long.

Procedure: Hang up the pairs as shown in the drawing, fig. 6–5. Start the workers from the middle pin, taking in the passives as you go along. After five cloth stitches with the two workers respectively, twist the workers once, and pass through another four pairs with cloth stitches. Twist the workers once, then pass them round the pins with half-stitches, pin, and half-stitch. Continue with cloth stitches out towards the braid through two passives with the same workers. Twist once, pass them through to the braid pins with double cloth stitch and pin, then carry straight on to the cloth stitch grounds with cloth stitches.

Fig. 6–4. Karin, designed and executed by Hildur Kratz.

Fig. 6–5. Work drawing. Double lines indicate beige, single lines white.

From the pins at the loose edges you get a new pair of workers which will pass first two beige passives, then one white and one beige pair, with cloth stitches. Turn round the pin, twisting the workers, and return towards the loose edge with cloth stitches. Follow the drawing for the irregular stitches in the brabant ground.

The spider begins with 16 cloth stitches.

Twist all the passives that go to the middle part of the spider once, but do not twist the beige ones. The workers from the loose edges meet in the middle of the spider with double cloth stitch, pin, cloth stitch, then go back to the loose edges, where you change to a new pair of workers to start another pattern section.

Fig. 6–7. Several squares can be joined together to form large sections for a tapestry or window screen.

Fig. 6–6. Pomona, designed and executed by Carina Ljungberg.

Pomona

This lace is rather complicated, and you have to stretch the cloth stitch ground well to achieve a good result.

Material: Linen yarn no. 25/3: 64 pairs of bobbins: weft yarn nos. 18/3 and 18/5, one thread of each spooled together: 3 pairs of bobbins.

Technique: Cloth stitch: torchon and brabant grounds: plaits: tallies: loose edges: gimp.

Size: 6¾ × 6¾ in. (16·2 × 16·2 cm.).

Procedure: Turn the pattern 90 degrees to the right. Spool the bobbins together two by two, and start the work with a closed braid. Put up the pairs as shown in the drawing, fig. 6–8, and begin the cloth stitch ground from the left, continuing it along the outer edges. The workers on the left side come straight from the upper cloth stitch ground, while passives from above continue as the workers on the right. Pass over at the same time to the torchon ground: the sequence for this is half-stitch, pin, half-stitch.

Continue the lace on the sides as far down as possible so that it is stable when the gimp comes in. Pass over to the large cloth stitch ground with two types of loose edges, one with a twist on the workers, the other with a twist on the passives. The plaits are done as follows: Cloth stitch, stretch, twist, cross, stretch, etc. In the next cloth stitch ground one of the plait pairs becomes the workers and enters from the right, at which point you bring in the gimp again. (See the section on separate insertion of threads in Chapter 9.)

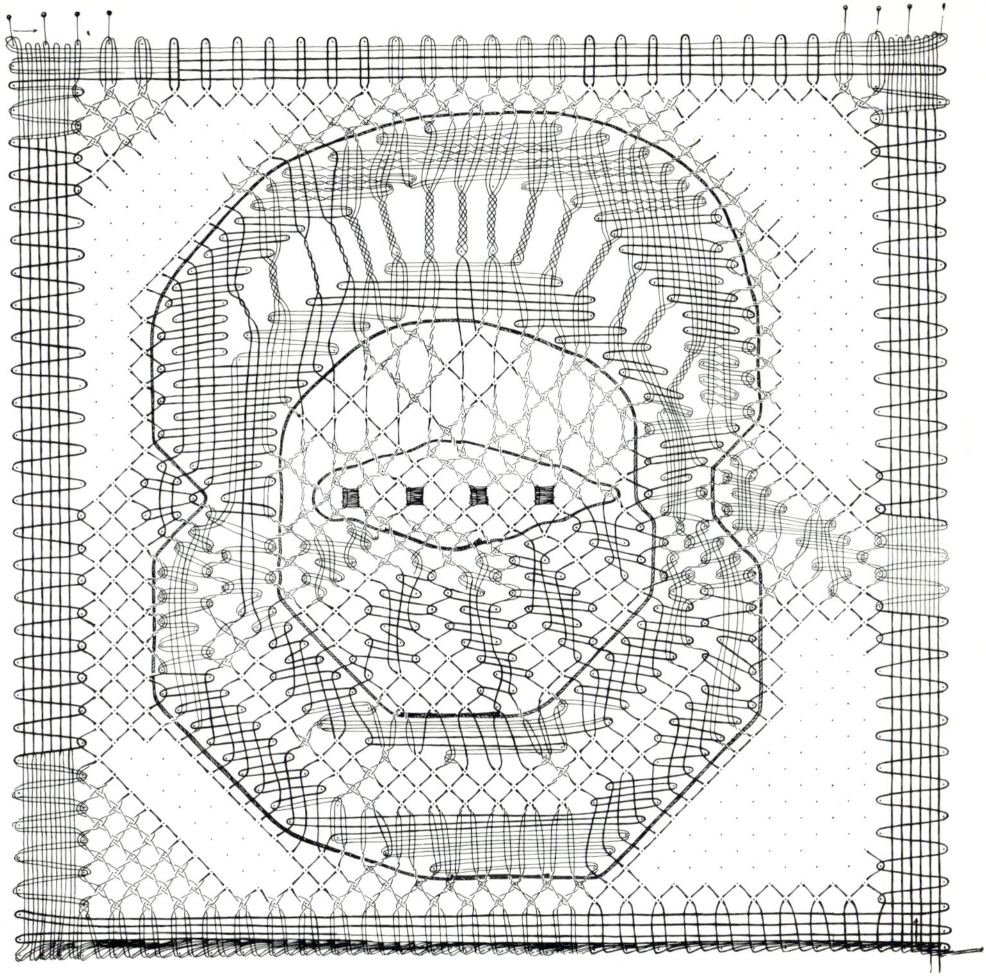

Fig. 6–8. Work drawing. Double lines show both threads in pairs where the lace is irregular, otherwise one line represents one pair.

Move to the brabant ground: the method is half-stitch, pin, half-stitch, twist. The weft inlay round the tallies also consists of double threads, which pass over each other in the joint. Make the tallies as shown in the drawing and explained in the section on tallies in Chapter 9. The pairs that pass in and out of the succeeding small cloth stitch grounds are only twisted once. Continue the lace according to the drawing, and finish-off in the same manner as 'Luna' in Chapter 3 (also described in the section on finishing-off in Chapter 9).

Opposite. Fig. 6–10. Pattern drawing in full scale. The insets are work details.

Pattern: Sketch on $\frac{1}{4}$ in. (6 mm.) square-ruled paper. A lengthening piece forms the beginning and the end of the lace-work. The part in between should be 19–20 in. (48–50 cm.) long to cover the reel. (See the section on separate pins in Chapter 9.) *Procedure:* Spool the bobbins together two by two. Start the lace in the middle of the lengthening piece. Put up the pairs as shown in the drawing, fig. 6–10, and begin the braid with cloth stitch ground which will be folded over when the lace is finished. Make cloth stitches all the way across the pattern from left to right. Make a row of pins where the lace is to be folded. Twist the passives once, then half-stitch, pin, half-stitch. Continue the cloth stitch ground up to the actual design. Twist the passives from the cloth stitch ground once before bringing them into the torchon ground with twists. The method for this ground is: Half-stitch, pin, half-stitch, extra twist.

Fig. 6–9. Sekora, designed and executed by Ann-Gritt Sekora.

Sekora

An even, coarse lace with a strict pattern is useful in many ways. This lace is neutral and non-disturbing, yet decorative as a small table-cloth or window-seat mat.
Material: Unbleached linen warp no. 8/2: 40 pairs of bobbins.
Technique: Cloth stitch ground: torchon ground with twists: picot with double cloth stitch.
Size: The lace is $7\frac{1}{2}$ in. (18 cm.) wide. One complete section of the pattern is 2 in. (4·8 cm.) long.

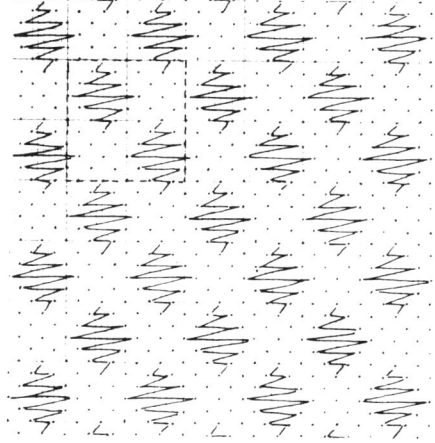

Fig. 6–11. Parts of the pattern surface.

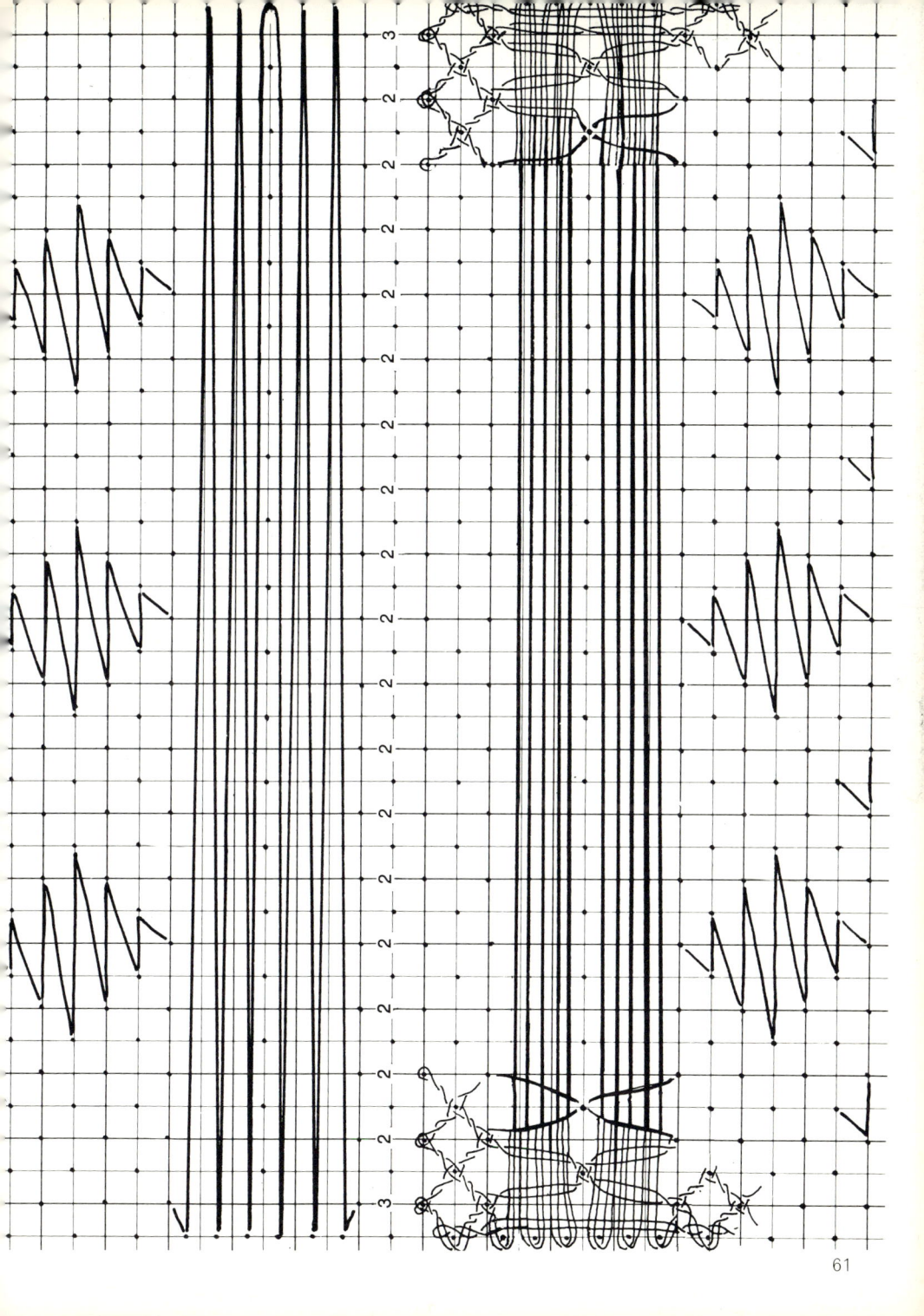

Do the picot as follows, the same on both sides: Double cloth stitch, pin, double cloth stitch, stretch. The workers pass from right to left in the cloth stitch ground. Give an extra twist to the pairs moving from this ground to the torchon ground with twists. Make the lace as long as desired before you finish with the same cloth stitch ground as in the beginning. Tie the pairs together before cutting off the threads, fold the ends under the hem, and cast-off by hand.

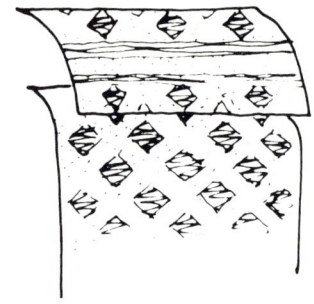

Fig. 6–12. How to join the lengthening piece and the centre part of the pattern together.

Children's sketches for laces.

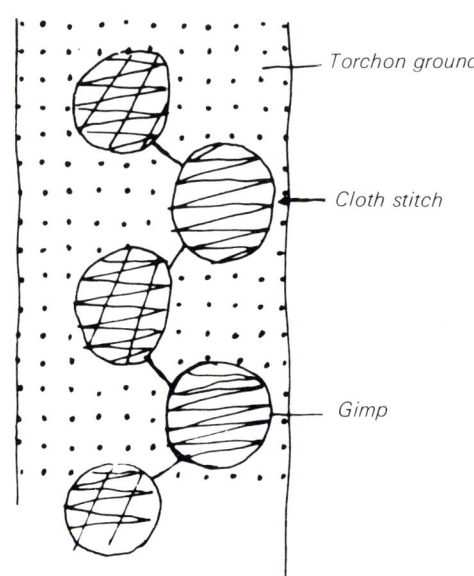

— Torchon ground

— Cloth stitch

— Gimp

7. Lace-play

After learning the different stitches and grounds you can experiment with various materials and techniques. This chapter describes some of the possibilities.

Box of diamonds

The lid for this box is decorated with a strict lace made from linen warp with cloth stitches. The warp is almost completely covered by the weft, giving the cloth stitch ground a striped appearance which is enhanced by the straight lines of the pin-holes.

The pattern is regular and can therefore be developed in many interesting ways. For example, you can distort it with a mirror. Many variations on the wedge pattern can be developed by placing a mirror alongside the braid. If you are joining two patterns remember to add half

Fig. 7–2. Box of diamonds, designed and executed by Wiwian Lundblad.

Fig. 7–1. Pattern drawing in full scale.

Fig. 7–3. Work drawing.

a square so that you can turn round when putting in the pins.

Material: Unbleached linen warp no. 8/2 or 6/2; 13 pairs of bobbins; brown wooden box with an unpainted lid 3 × $3\frac{3}{4}$ in. (7·2 × 9 cm.).

Technique: Cloth stitch.

Size: The lace is $2\frac{1}{2}$ in. (6 cm.) wide.

Pattern: Drawing in full scale on $\frac{1}{4}$ in. (6 mm.) square-ruled paper (fig. 7–1).

Procedure: Spool the bobbins together two by two. Put up the pairs as shown in the drawing, fig. 7–3. There are four workers in the lace; one for each of the diagonal grounds. Each ground has three passives. Make the grounds in the order shown in the drawing and the photograph, figs. 7–1 and 2. Give only one twist between the grounds. The braid is done as follows: Cloth stitch, pin, twist, cloth stitch. When the lace is finished tie the pairs together, and cut off the threads.

Fitting: Glue the lace to a piece of suede or linen, then glue this piece to the lid of the box, and push the threads under the edge of the lid.

Watch-strap

Material: White and green plaited nylon line; 4 pairs of bobbins; metal buckle 1 × $1\frac{1}{2}$ in. (2·4 × 3·6 cm.).

Technique: Cloth stitch.

Size: The strap is $\frac{1}{2}$ in. (1·2 cm.) wide. The length is the circumference of your wrist plus 2 in. (4·8 cm.).

Pattern: Drawing on $\frac{1}{4}$ in. (6 mm.) square-ruled paper or chequered fabric.

Procedure: Spool the bobbins together two by two. You need about 2 yd. (2 m.) of line for the workers and about 1 yd. (1 m.) for the other pairs. Fasten the lines to the buckle with headings; put the buckle on the reel. Using the pair to the far right as the workers, make cloth stitches with twists wherever you put down the pins. Make the strap as long as necessary. When it is finished take it off the reel. Fold a piece of metal foil round the edge of the strap, melt the line ends together with a warm iron, and shape them to the desired form.

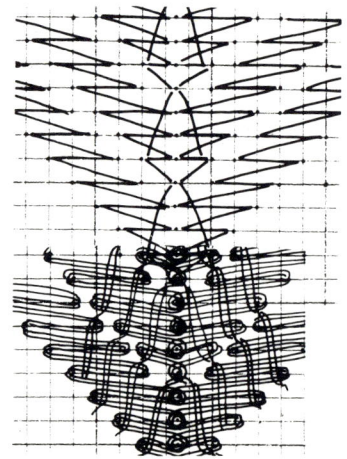

Fig. 7–4. Pattern variation. With the help of a mirror you can alter the pattern in many ways.

7.

Colour plate 7. Lapland huts.
This lace is described on
p. 49.

Colour plate 8. Striped
curtain. This lace is
described on p. 7.

8.

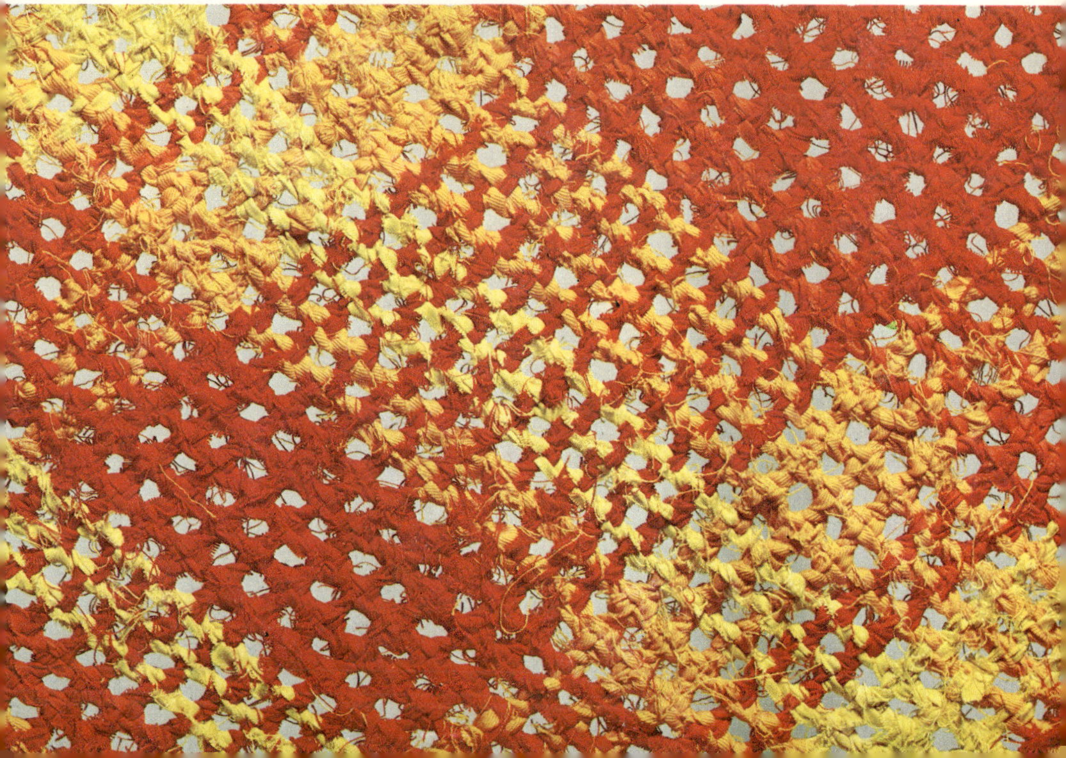

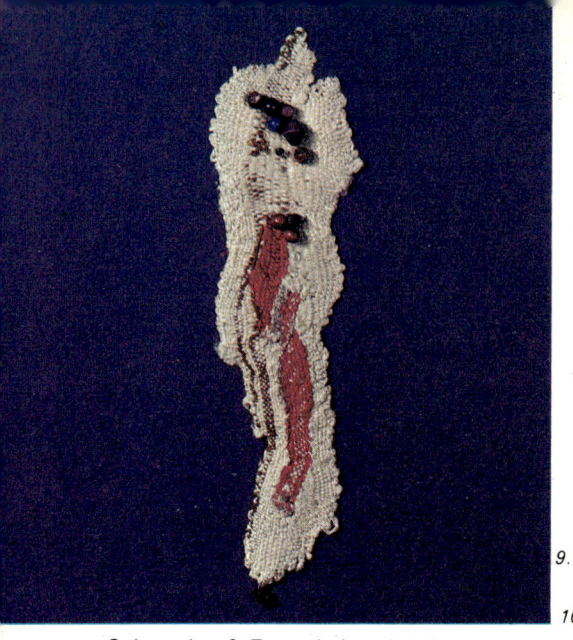

9.

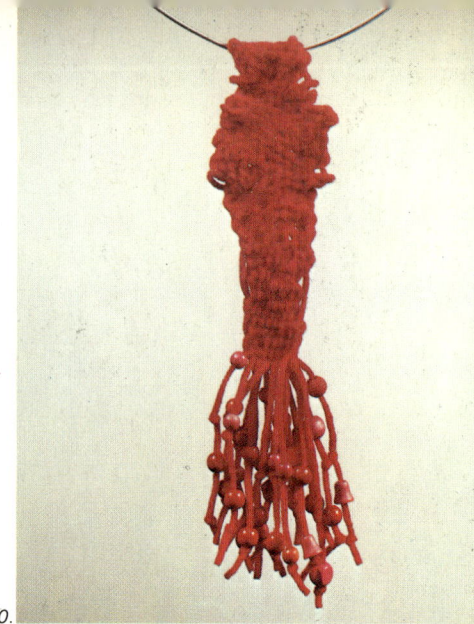

10.

Colour plate 9. Tatta, designed and executed by Ulla Bladh. This lace is made with cloth stitches alone from unbleached linen yarn, green and violet cotton, thin silver threads, wooden and glass beads.

Colour plate 10. Bark pendant, designed and executed by Christina Jangrell. The materials for this lace are velvet yarn and wooden beads, and it is made with cloth stitches.

11.

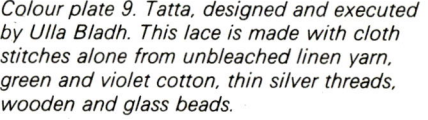

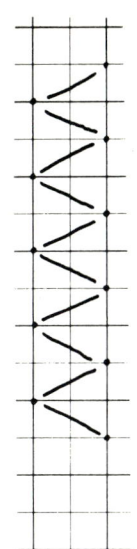

Fig. 7–5. Work drawing.

Fig. 7–6. Pattern drawing in full scale.

Fig. 7–7. How to fasten the threads round the buckle.

Fig. 7–8. Watch-strap, designed and executed by Inga-Märit Gottås and Wiweca Forsberg.

Colour plate 11. a. and b. Woven pendants. c. Glass bead pendant. d. Wooden bead pendant. All of these laces are described on pp. 79, 80, and 81.

*Fig. 7–9. Treasure chest,
designed and executed
by Ingrid Parving-Olsson.*

Treasure chest

Material: Rayon rope: 9 pairs of bobbins:
dyed wood chips: wooden beads.

Technique: Cloth stitch: torchon ground.

Size: $4\frac{1}{2}$ × 6 in. (10·8 × 14·4 cm.).

Pattern: Drawing on $\frac{1}{4}$ in. (6 mm.) square-
ruled paper.

Procedure: Spool the pairs together two by
two. (The rope should be damp.) The
workers need more rope than the other
pairs. Thread the beads on the warp
threads. Straighten the wood chips by
dampening them, then cut them into $2\frac{1}{4}$ ×
$\frac{1}{4}$ in. (5·4 × 6 mm.) pieces. The chips come
into the lace on the weft yarn. The beads go
on top of the chips as shown in the

drawing and the photograph, figs. 7–8 and
10. Twist the workers twice in the cloth
stitch ground, as indicated in the pattern.

Fitting: Finish-off with reef knots (fig. 7–9).
Paint or stain the box before you glue the
lace on the lid.

Fig. 7–11. Reef knot.

66

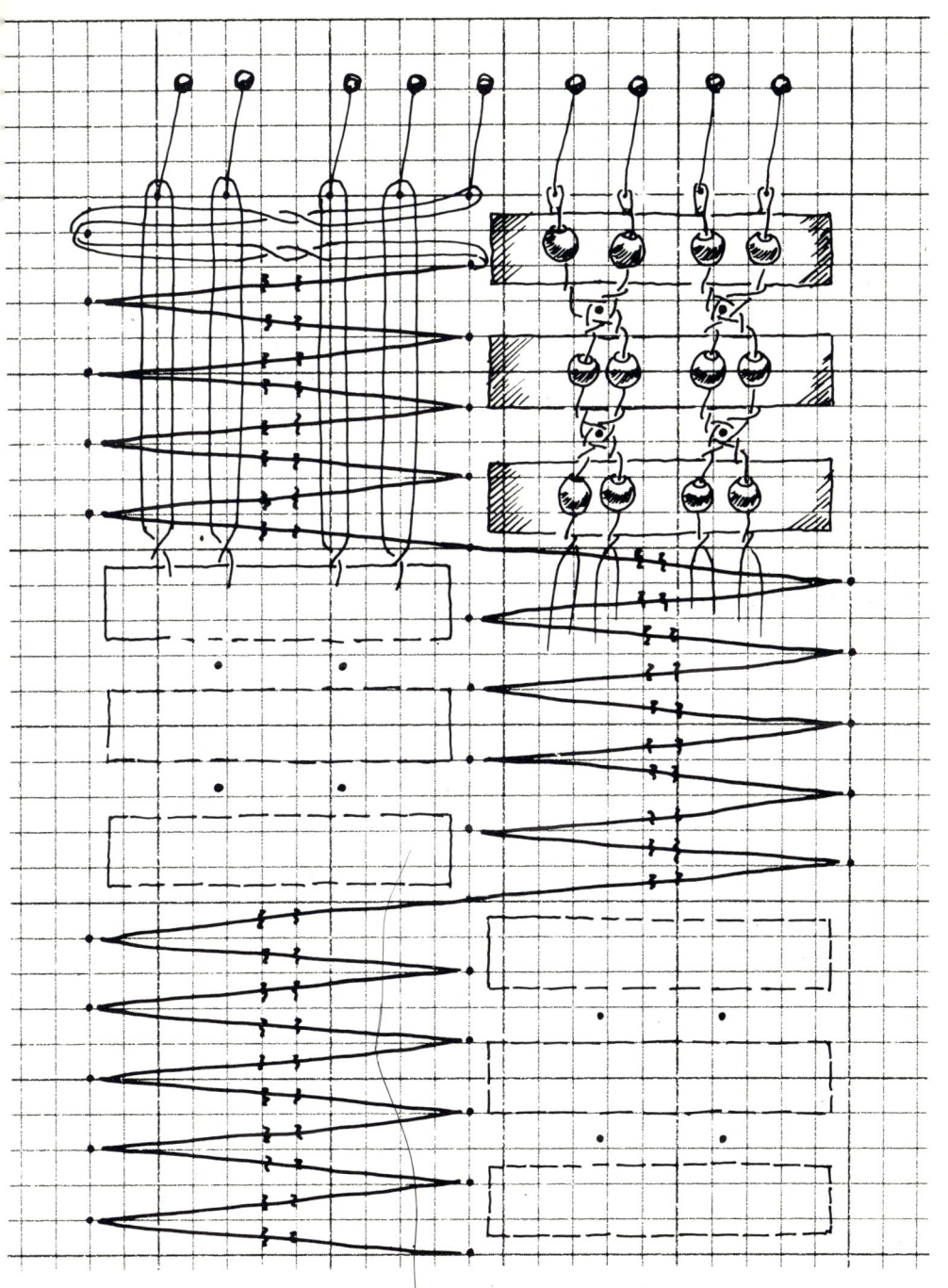

Fig. 7–10. Pattern drawing in full scale.

*Fig. 7–12. Purse face,
designed and executed
by Dagmar Sjödin
and Barbro Westin.*

Purse face

This simple lace is designed for children in primary school. It can be stitched on a purse sewn by the child, or you can put it on a pocket or a bag. An adult can make it in one and a half hours.

Material: Cotton yarn: 10 pairs of bobbins: 2 metal rings.

Technique: Cloth stitch.

Size: $2\frac{1}{4}$ × $2\frac{1}{2}$ in. (5·4 × 6 cm.).

Pattern: Drawing on $\frac{1}{4}$ in. (6 mm.) square-ruled paper.

Procedure: The face is made upside down, starting with the chin. Spool the bobbins together two by two to get a closed braid. Make a cloth stitch with an extra twist when turning. Following the drawing, fig. 7–14, divide the pairs in half for the mouth. Note that the new workers take a supporting pin and a twist. Continue the cloth stitches on both sides to fasten the ear-rings, as shown in the detailed sketch, fig. 7–15. Divide the pairs, putting four in the middle and three on each side, for the eyes. These new workers also take a supporting pin and a twist. Finish the lace with a closed braid, making three cloth stitches. Remove the workers by passing them through four pairs and then out. Continue removing pairs until they are all turned upwards over the face. Cut off the threads to form the hair, and sew in extra threads if necessary.

Fitting: The face is fitted on a piece of suede (the front of the purse). The back is also a piece of suede the same size. Sew the two pieces together with velcrum ribbon.

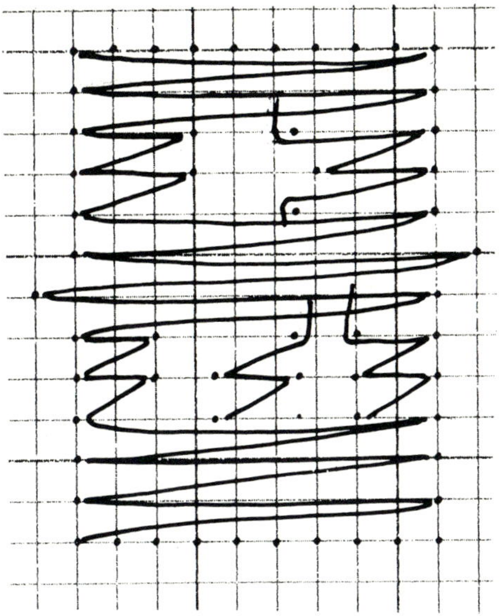

Fig. 7–13. Pattern drawing in full scale.

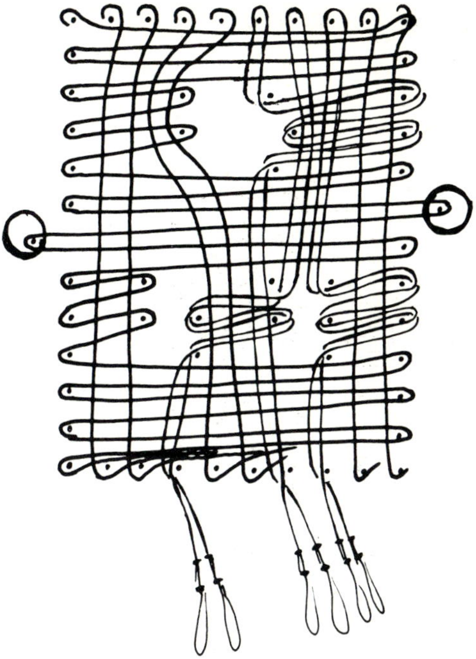

Fig. 7–14. Work drawing.

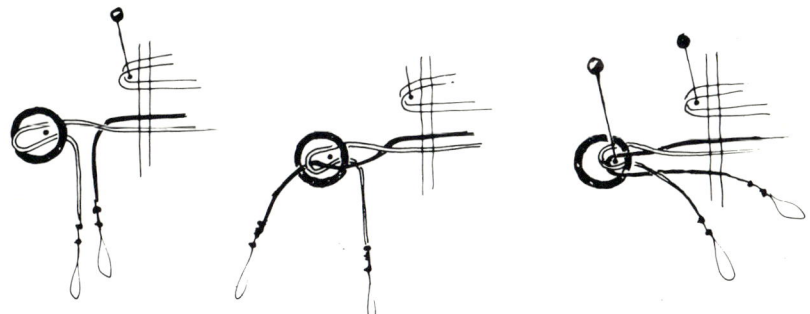

Fig. 7–15. How to fasten the metal ring to the lace.

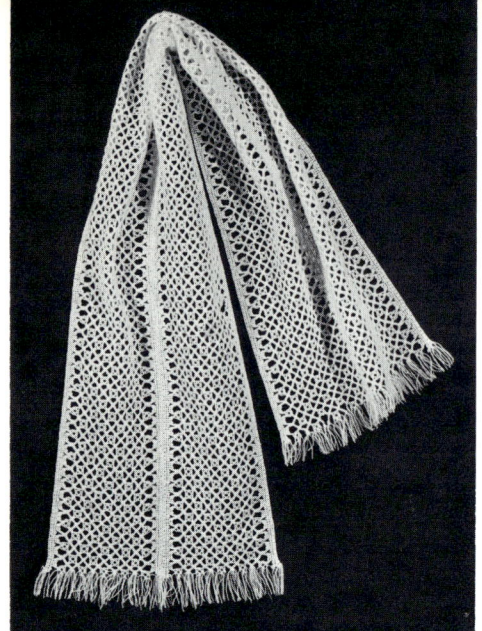

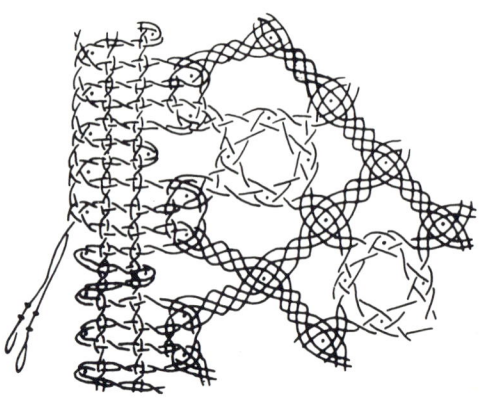

Fig. 7–17. Work drawing.

Fig. 7–16. Rose ground shawl, designed and
executed by Olle Norin.

Rose ground shawl

Material: Thin white two-ply mohair yarn:
42 pairs of bobbins.
Technique: Plaits: rose ground: broad
edge with double cloth stitch.
Size: One section is about $6\frac{1}{4}$ in. (15 cm.)
wide. The entire shawl with fringe is $12\frac{1}{4}$ ×
52 in. (29 × 125 cm.).

Pattern: Drawing on $\frac{1}{4}$ in. (6 mm.) square-
ruled paper.
Procedure: Make the plaits wide and
rather loose. The stretching will turn out
even if you start with a cloth stitch, then
stretch, twist, cross, and stretch again.

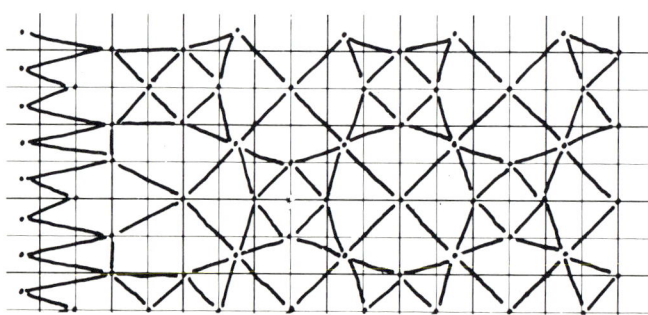

Fig. 7–18. Pattern drawing
in full scale.

8. Jewelry and accessories

This aspect of lace making also allows wide latitude to your imagination. Many of the laces are suitable for beginners, since they use only cloth stitch, varying it with different placings of the pins and many colours.

Puzzle piece

This motif is a nice ornament for a plain pocket or a bag. It takes two hours to make. The material of the lace and the article to be decorated must be equally stretchable.
Material: Three shades of red wool: 9 pairs of bobbins.
Technique: Cloth stitch and twists.
Size: 4½ × 4½ in. (10·8 × 10·8 cm.).
Pattern: Free-form drawing.
Procedure: Spool the bobbins together two by two. The first two workers need 6½ yd. (6 m.) of yarn and the other pairs 2 yd. (2 m.) each. The lace is made with cloth stitch, twisting once when turning. Make additional twists in the cloth stitch ground to give a loose effect. Bring in new workers in the middle of the motif. When you reach the hole, put two pairs to the left and three pairs to the right of it. The new workers to the left become passives later on, as shown in the drawing, fig. 8–2.
Fitting: Fasten the hanging threads to the back of the lace. Pin the work to the garment in question and cast-on with a thread of the same colour as the lace.

Fig. 8–1. Puzzle piece, designed and executed by Ann-Catherine Svensson and Kerstin Stridh.

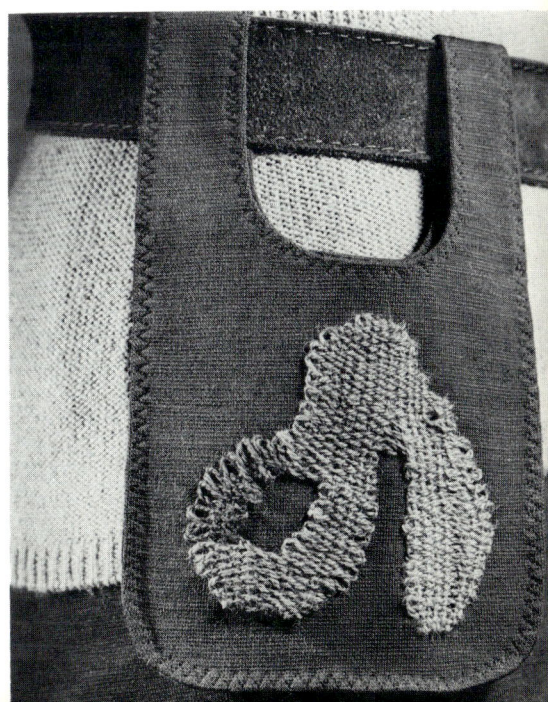

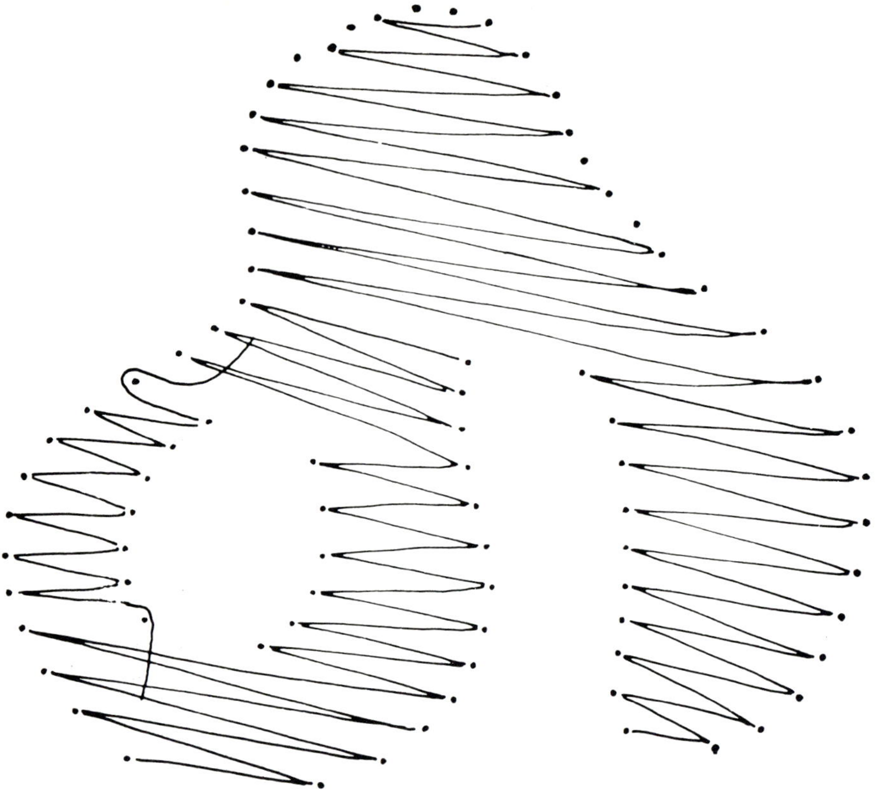

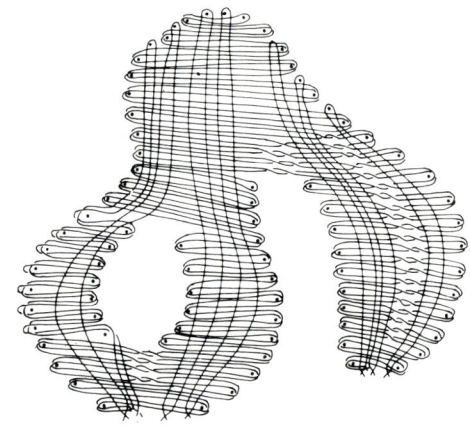

Fig. 8–2. Pattern drawing in full scale.

Fig. 8–4. The decoration is made of two-ply wool.

Fig. 8–3. Work drawing. Note the extra twist with the workers when putting a pin in the roundest part of the lower circle.

Belt

It takes about an hour to make this beautiful belt in coarse fishing line, which is available in a range of attractive colours. The slight elasticity of the line is ideal for a soft belt that follows the shape of the waist.

Material: Dyed fishing line no. 8/2: 6 pairs of bobbins; 6 coloured wooden beads $\frac{3}{4}$ in. (1·8 cm.) in diameter.

Technique: Half-stitch ground; plaits.

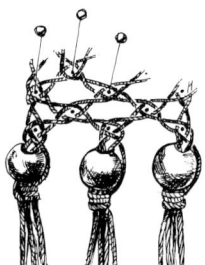

Fig. 8–5. Detail of the end piece with half-stitch ground, beads, and knots.

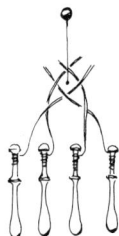

Fig. 8–6. Detail of a half-stitch round a pin.

Fig. 8–7. Detail of the plait with a half-stitch.

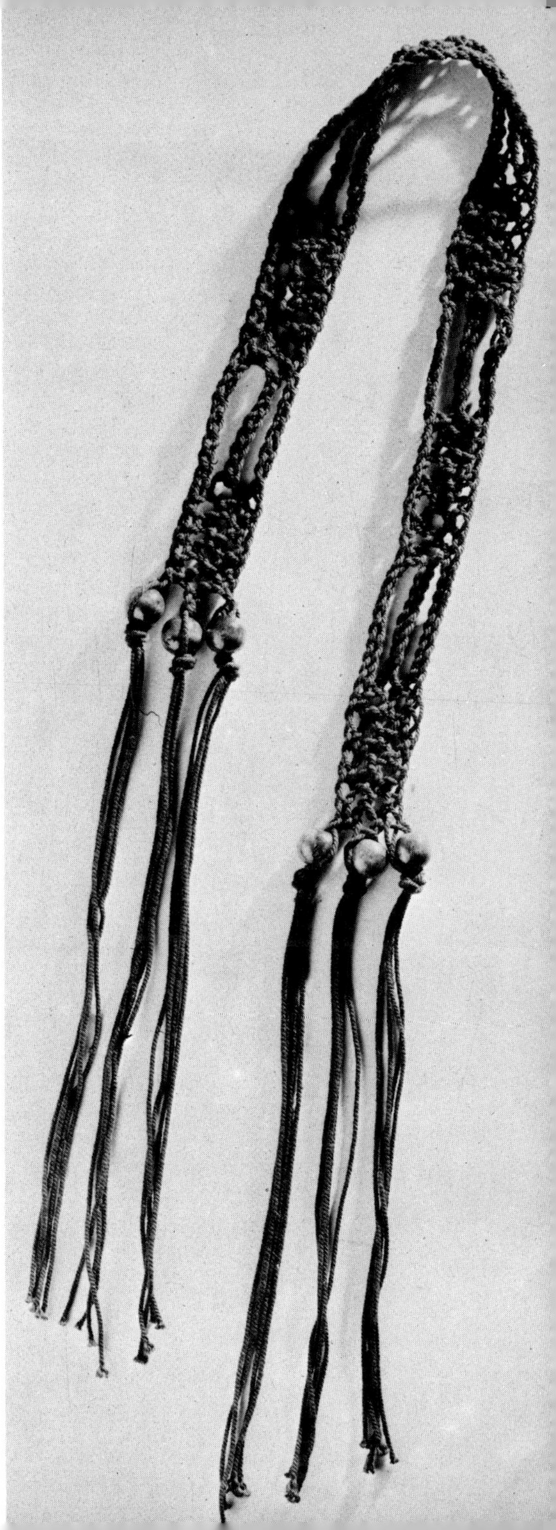

Fig. 8–8. Belt, designed and executed by Eva-Lotta Eriksson.

Fig. 8–9. Belt (detail).

a detail of repeating pattern

Fig. 8–10. Pattern drawing in full scale.

Size: 1¾ in. (4·2 cm.) wide and 22 in. (55 cm.) long, with 12 in. (28·8 cm.) fringe on each side.

Pattern: Drawing on ¼ in. (6 mm.) square-ruled paper.

Procedure: Spool about 2 yd. (2 m.) of line on the bobbins one by one, and tie them together in pairs, letting the fringe hang loose. Pin each knot on the pattern according to the drawing, fig. 8–5. Make a ground 2 in. (4·8 cm.) long with half-stitches but no extra twists when turning, and pin where marked on the drawing.

Next half-stitch three round plaits of four threads in this order: cross, twist, stretch, cross, twist, and stretch. This section is also 2 in. (4·8 cm.) long. Alternate these two parts until the belt is long enough. Finish-off with a half-stitch ground as in the beginning. Tie the pairs together, and fasten a wooden bead on each knot. The threads hanging loose form the fringe.

74

Bead belt

Material: Synthetic grey rope; 5 pairs of bobbins; silver wooden beads $\frac{1}{4}$ in. (6 mm.) in diameter; silver metal buckle.

Technique: Cloth stitch.

Size: $1\frac{1}{2}$ × 26 in. (3·6 × 65 cm.).

Pattern: Drawing on $\frac{1}{4}$ in. (6 mm.) square-ruled paper.

Procedure: Thread the beads on the three centre passives. The beads are distributed successively in the cloth stitch ground, as shown in the drawing, fig. 8–11. Start and finish with a $1\frac{1}{2}$ in. (3·6 cm.) plain cloth stitch ground. These edges are folded round the buckle. The rope is easier to work with if you dampen it as you go along.

Fitting: Tie the ends together in reef knots. Fasten the buckle to the belt.

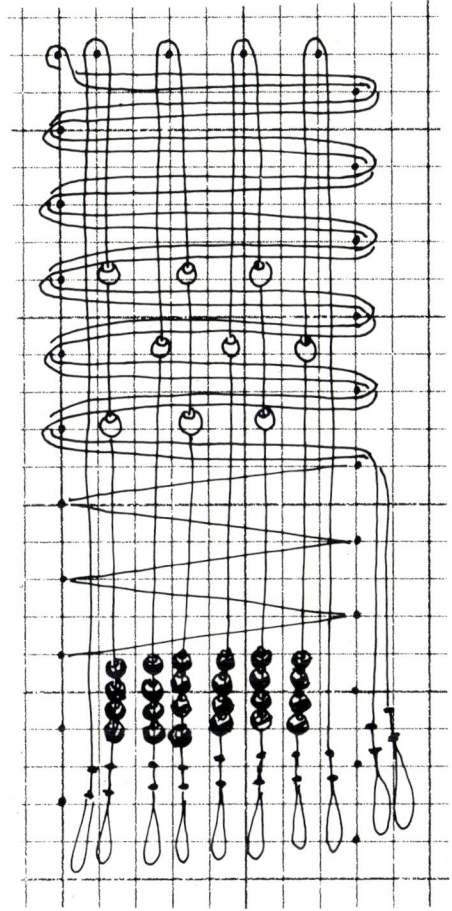

Fig. 8–11. Pattern drawing in full scale.

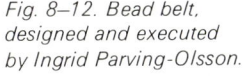

Fig. 8–12. Bead belt, designed and executed by Ingrid Parving-Olsson.

Fig. 8–13. Queen of the forest, designed and executed by Ingrid Parving-Olsson.

take away an extra pair here

Queen of the forest

Spruce, birch, and pine: materials from the forest are easy to combine with textiles. Wooden beads and pieces of birch bark give form and stability to the necklace, which is tied round the neck with a cord. *Material:* Shimmering grey linen yarn no. 35/2: 6 pairs of bobbins: birch bark: uncoloured pine beads $\frac{1}{8}$ in. (3 mm.) in diameter.
Technique: Cloth stitch: gimp (for the pieces of bark).

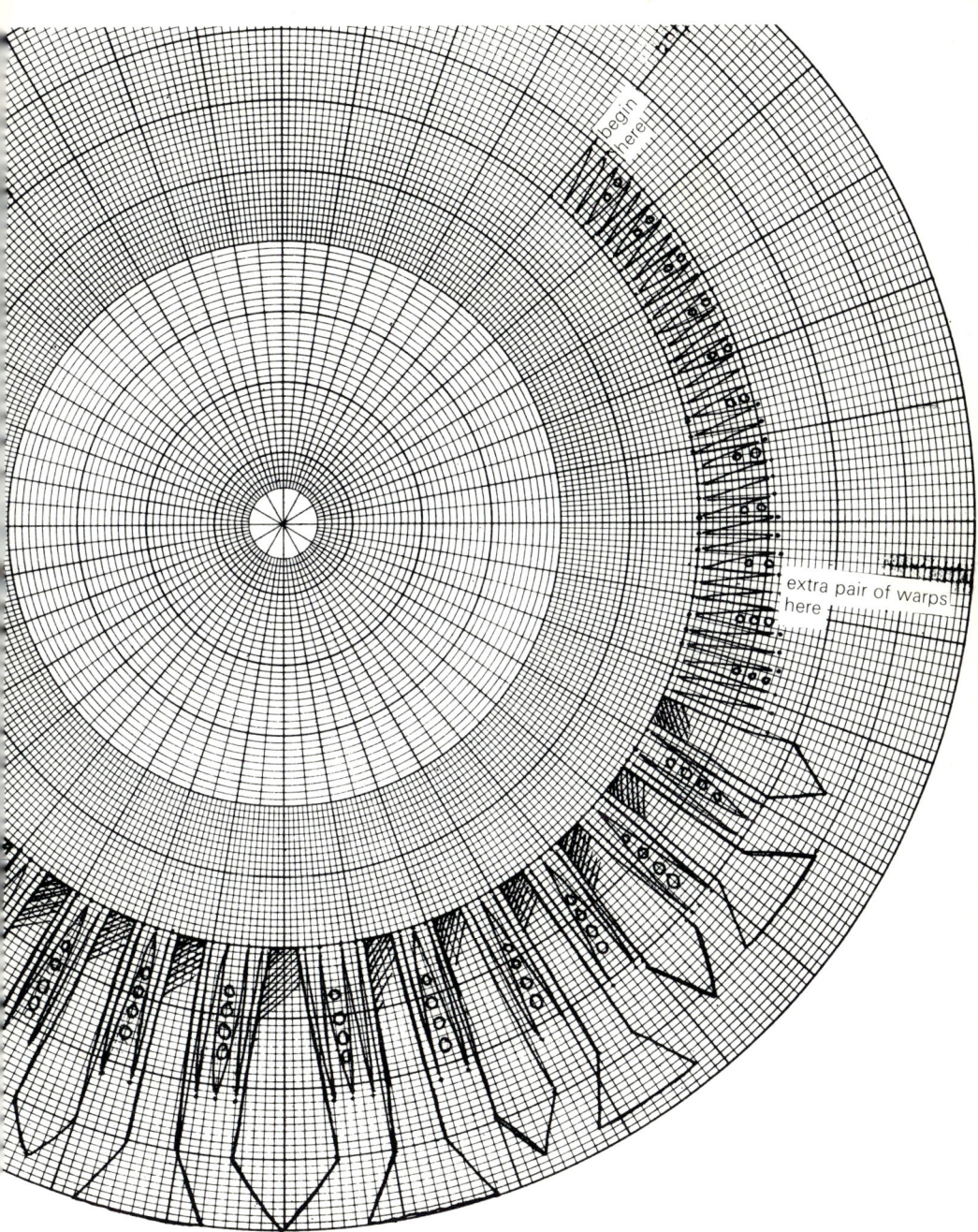

Fig. 8–14. Pattern drawing in full scale.

begin here

extra pair of warps here

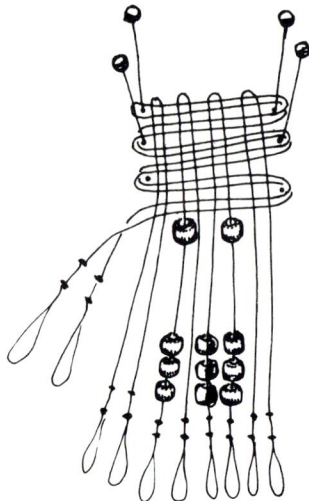

Fig. 8–15. Detail of putting up the bobbins. Note that only three pairs carry beads in the beginning.

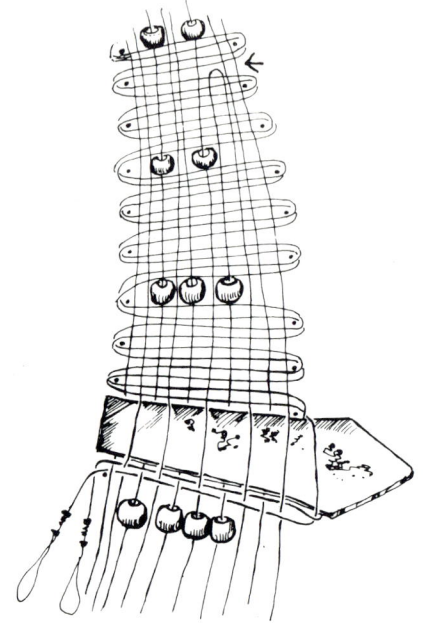

Fig. 8–17. Detail to show how the extra bead pair comes in. Put in an extra pin here.

Fig. 8–16. The necklace is tied round the neck.

Size: 14½ in. (36 cm.) long, ⅞ in. (2 cm.) wide.

Pattern: Drawing on circular square-ruled paper.

Procedure: Spool the bobbins together two by two, giving more yarn to the workers than to the other pairs. Thread the beads on four of the bobbins, as in the drawing, fig. 8–17. One of these pairs does not come in until the necklace is broadened in the middle. Make the cloth stitch ground from side to side, bringing in the beads as shown in the pattern. The bark comes in as gimp. When the workers pass along the upper edge the bark pieces move left, and when the workers return on the other side the thread nearest to the bark must return in the original direction of the bobbins. (This is necessary for the warp threads to pass straight over the birch bark.)

Fitting: Finish the lace with small reef knots. Fold them inside, and fasten them. Glue the warp threads to the backs of the bark pieces all the way round the necklace. Attach two cords to the ends of the necklace for tying.

Fig. 8–18. a. Glass bead pendant, designed and executed by Ina Gunnarsdotter-Malmsten. b. Wooden bead pendant, designed and executed by Ann-Mari Svending. See colour plate 11, opposite p. 65.

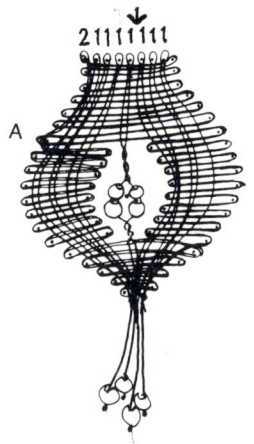

Fig. 8–19. Work drawing for wooden bead pendant.

Fig. 8–20. Detail showing how to turn round a pin while keeping the right colour.

Wooden bead pendant

Material: Linen yarn or weaving linen no. 16/2 in a red or blue shade: 9 pairs of bobbins: 22 small wooden beads $\frac{1}{4}$ in. (6 mm.) in diameter in the same shades as the yarn: leather for fitting.
Technique: Cloth stitch.
Size: $1\frac{3}{4} \times 2\frac{1}{4}$ in. ($4 \cdot 2 \times 5 \cdot 4$ cm.).
Pattern: Drawing on $\frac{1}{4}$ in. (6 mm.) square-ruled paper.

Fig. 8–21. Pattern drawing in full scale for wooden bead pendant.

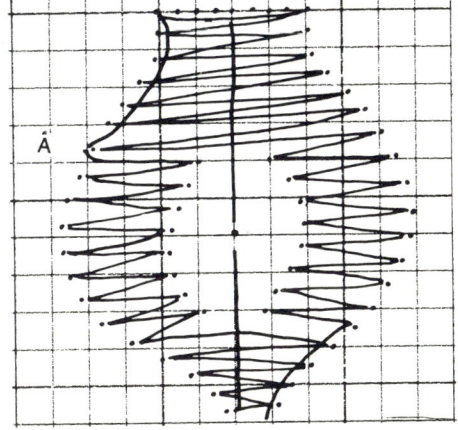

Procedure: Spool the bobbins together two by two so the lace starts with a closed braid. One of the pairs carries two beads on each thread. Put up the bobbins as shown in the drawing, fig. 8–19, with the bead pair in the centre, and make cloth stitches from left to right. Give an extra twist to the workers when you put in a pin.

When you come to the hole in the middle divide the bobbins in half (four pairs on each side), leaving the bead pair in the middle. The outer pair on the left becomes the new workers. Twist the bead pair a few times, put in a pin, and twist it again a few times. Continue the cloth stitches. The pair on the left remains the workers throughout the rest of the lace, and the original workers pair on the right becomes passive, as indicated in the drawing, fig. 8–21. End the lace in a point.

Gather the warp threads together, and tie the threads from the workers round them. Fasten the worker threads on the back of the pendant. Cut the warp threads to different lengths, thread on the beads, and knot them.

Fitting: Glue the pendant on a piece of leather slightly smaller than the lace itself. Plait a long cord in the same linen yarn as the lace for tying the pendant round the neck.

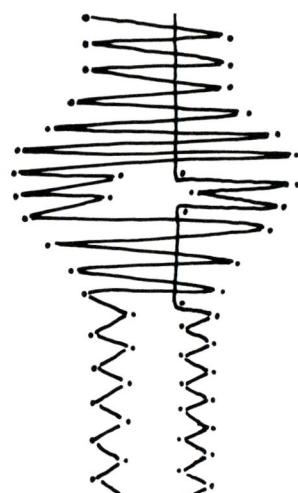

Fig. 8–22. Pattern drawing in full scale for scale for glass bead pendant.

Fig. 8–23. Work drawing for glass bead pendant.

Glass bead pendant

Material: Unbleached linen yarn or weaving linen no. 16/2; 9 pairs of bobbins; brown and gold glass beads; leather for fitting.

Technique: Cloth stitch; twists.

Size: $1\frac{1}{2}$ × $2\frac{3}{4}$ in. (3·6 × 6·6 cm.) without the fringe.

Pattern: Drawing in full scale.

Procedure: Spool the bobbins together two by two so the lace begins with a closed braid. Start with the widest part of the lace, which will be the lower end when the pendant is finished. The lace is a single cloth stitch ground; begin in the upper left-hand corner. Give the usual extra twist to the workers when putting in a pin. To achieve the loose effect in the centre, divide the ground in two, bring in new workers from the passives, as shown in the drawing, fig. 8–23, and give one, two, or three extra twists to the workers in the middle.

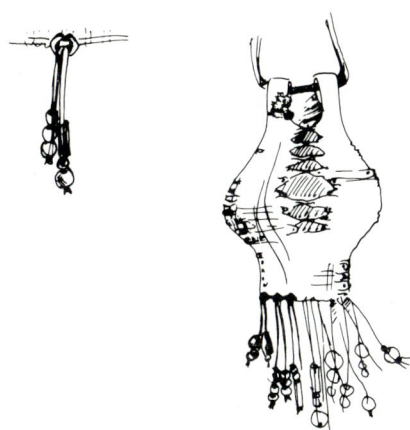

Fig. 8–24. How the fringe with beads is attached to the pendant.

Make the long and thin grounds separately. Tie the threads together two by two with reef knots, keeping one thread to fasten with.
Fitting: The pendant is glued to a piece of leather somewhat smaller than the lace itself. String the glass beads on a number of threads, and fasten them in the lower braid as shown in fig. 8–24. Fold the top pieces of the lace into loops, and fasten them on the back. Thread a leather string through the loops for hanging the pendant round the neck.

Woven pendant

Material: Cotton yarn for hem-stitching: 10 pairs of bobbins: small wooden beads.
Technique: Cloth stitch with twists (in accordance with the indications in the pattern, fig. 8–26).
Size: $1\frac{3}{4}$ × $1\frac{3}{4}$ in. (4·2 × 4·2 cm.).
Pattern: Drawing in full scale on $\frac{1}{4}$ in. (6 mm.) square-ruled paper.
Procedure: Spool the bobbins together two by two, giving the workers more yarn than the others. Put the workers and seven passive pairs in the upper row of pins, and make cloth stitches from side to side. Bring in a new pair on each side as shown in the drawing, fig. 8–27. The wavy strokes indicate the twists.

Fig. 8–25. a. and b. Woven pendants, designed and executed by Ingrid Parving-Olsson. Both are made from the same pattern. See colour plate 11, opposite p. 65.

Fitting: Tie the threads together with reef knots. Thread the beads on the yarn ends, and knot them. The fringe can either be uneven or even (fig. 8–25, a and b).

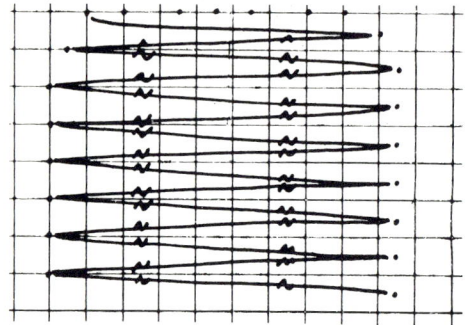

Fig. 8–26. Pattern drawing in full scale.

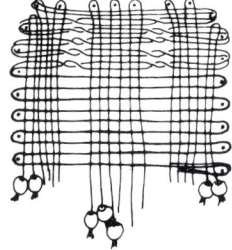

Fig. 8–27. Work drawing.

Purse

The coarse lace used for this purse is Fields with squares.

Material: Unbleached linen warp no. 8/3; 16 pairs of bobbins.

Technique: Cloth stitch; open edge braid; half-stitch in the middle of the square.

Size: The lace is $3\frac{1}{2}$ in. (8·4 cm.) wide. One complete section of the pattern is $2\frac{3}{4}$ in. (6·6 cm.) long. The finished purse measures $3 \times 3\frac{1}{2}$ in. (7·2 × 8·4 cm.).

Procedure: Use coarse bobbins for this material since it must be well stretched. Put in the pins as shown in the diagram, fig. 8–29. The digits indicate the number of pairs.

To strengthen the lace on the borders of the cloth stitch ground, change workers each time you put in a pin. Make the cloth stitches beside the pin, and stretch hard.

Note that the workers coming from within the lace must be twisted before moving out to the braid. The braid consists of a single double cloth stitch, but you must put in a pin between the second and third pairs to achieve a straight braid.

Fitting: You need two squares of brown suede $3\frac{1}{2} \times 5\frac{1}{2}$ in. (8·4 × 13·2 cm.), a bag frame, and a needle for working in leather. Stitch closely along the shorter sides of the lace so that it will not fray. Fold the lace double with the inner side out, and stitch the edges together, leaving 1 in. (2·4 cm.) open at the top for the frame. Turn it inside-out, and press the seams.

The suede lining is somewhat smaller than the outer lace part. Fold the skin with the suede side out, and stitch the sides together close to the edge with silk thread, leaving 1 in. (2·4 cm.) open at the top. Put the lining inside the lace bag and stitch the layers together. Attach the finished bag to the frame, and sew through the holes with the same linen yarn used for the lace.

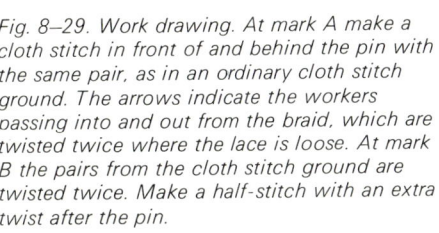

Fig. 8–28. Purse, designed by Siv Haraldsson and Naime Thorlin and executed by Signe Andersson.

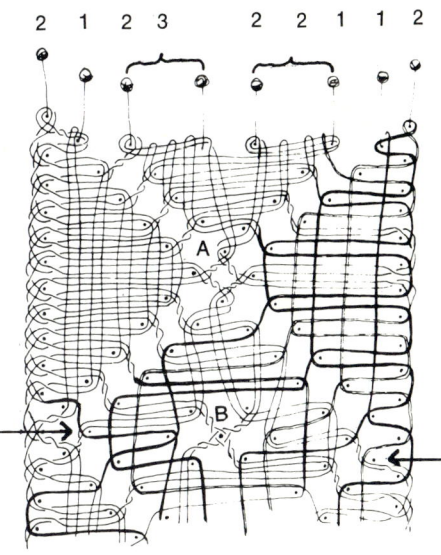

Fig. 8–29. Work drawing. At mark A make a cloth stitch in front of and behind the pin with the same pair, as in an ordinary cloth stitch ground. The arrows indicate the workers passing into and out from the braid, which are twisted twice where the lace is loose. At mark B the pairs from the cloth stitch ground are twisted twice. Make a half-stitch with an extra twist after the pin.

Fig. 8–30. Carrier bag, designed and executed by Kasja Borg.

Carrier bag

This useful everyday bag will hold an A4 size file, the evening paper, and some shopping. It is made of strong canvas linen and is decorated with leather strings. Leather is not a difficult material to work with, and you do not have to stretch so much in this loose ground.

Material: About 27 yd. (25 m.) of leather lacing; 14 pairs of coarse bobbins; 14 brown beads $\frac{1}{2}$ in. (1·2 cm.) in diameter

Technique: Net ground.

Size: One section is 5 × 2$\frac{1}{2}$ in. (12 × 6 cm.). The entire figure is 9$\frac{1}{4}$ × 5$\frac{1}{2}$ in. (22 × 13·2 cm.). At one side the lace work is slightly drawn together; on the other side the beads are added in the seam.

Pattern: Drawing in full scale on $\frac{1}{4}$ in. (6 mm.) square-ruled paper.

Procedure: Wind the leather lacing on the bobbins. The entire lace is made with half-stitches, and no extra twists are needed.

Make four sections, as shown in the drawing, fig. 8–31.

Fitting: Tie the pairs together at the ends. Arrange the sections as in the photograph, fig. 8–30. Thread the beads on one string from each section to hide the seam, and tie the sections together. Stitch the figure on the bag with brown cotton.

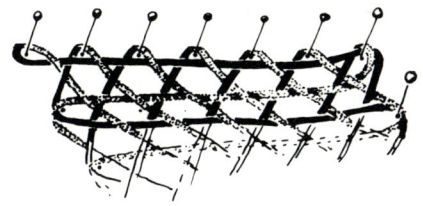

Fig. 8–32. Detail of work drawing.

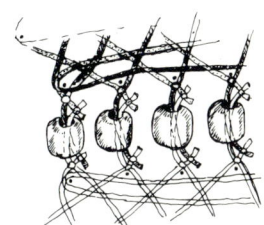

Fig. 8–33. Detail of pattern drawing, showing how the pieces are joined together.

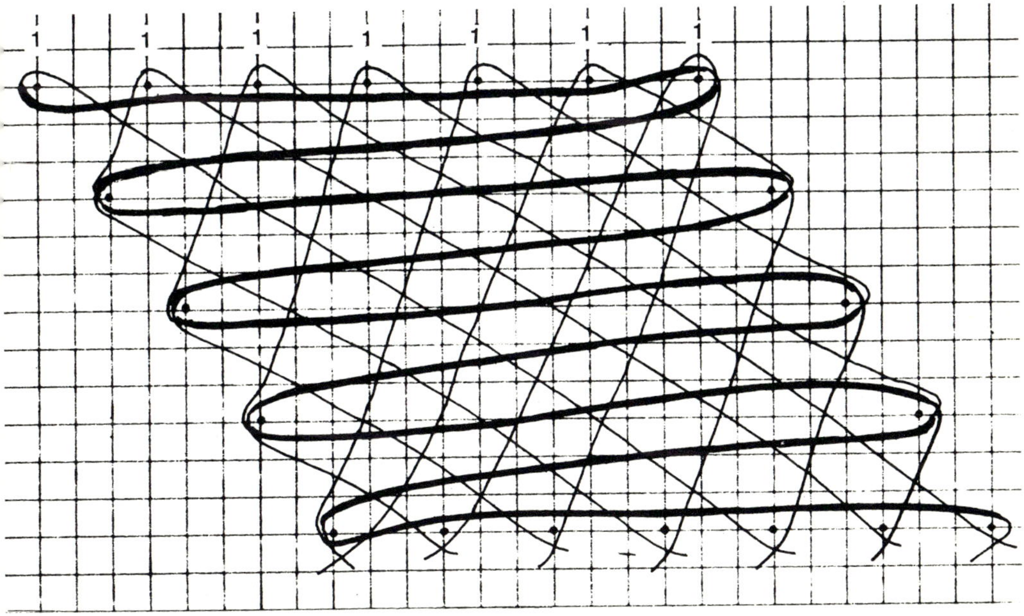

Fig. 8–31. Pattern and work drawing in full scale. Note that two sections represent the back of the pattern.

9. Techniques and methods

This chapter covers both technical points and working instructions. Basic movements have had to be repeated, with the addition of some new grounds. The technical details provided may be found of general interest in spite of the limited examples. With such details beside him, anyone wishing to try out his own methods would be well advised not to alter either the material or the technique of those designs for which instructions have been detailed. The last part of the chapter includes instructions for lace mounting.

Loop

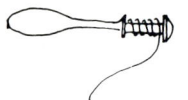 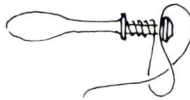 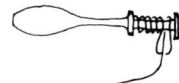

Fig. 9–1. Loop. It is easier to pass a thread under the lace work if you loop it round the bobbin.

Basic movements

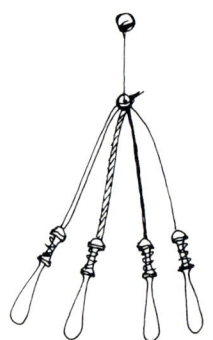

Fig. 9–2. Starting position of the bobbins.

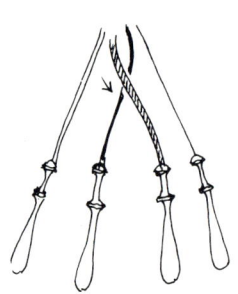

Fig. 9–3. Cross.

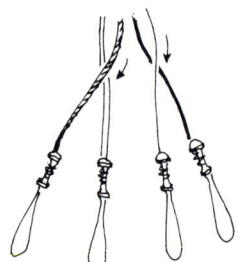

Fig. 9–4. Twist.

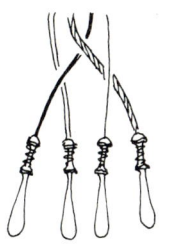 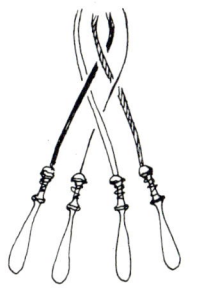 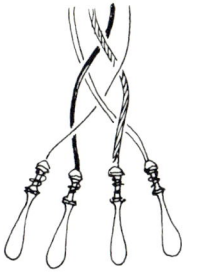 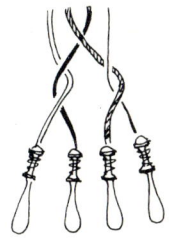

Fig. 9–5. Half-stitch: Cross, twist.

Fig. 9–6. Whole stitch. Cross, twist, cross.

Fig. 9–7. Double stitch: Cross, twist, cross, twist.

Fig. 9–8. Half-stitch with an extra twist: Pass in front of the net ground with a twist.

Inserting the gimp

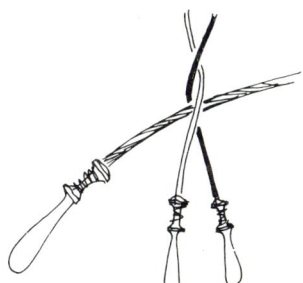 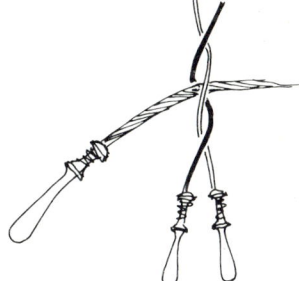

Fig. 9–9. The gimp entering from the left.

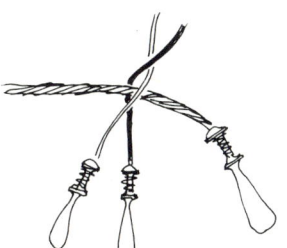

Fig. 9–10. The gimp entering from the right.

Edges

Fig. 9–11. Common edge: Double stitch, double stitch, extra twist on the outermost pair, pin, double stitch.

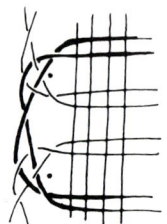

Fig. 9–12. Open pin edge: Pass in front of the points shown in the drawing.

Putting up bobbins diagonally

Fig. 9–13. Putting up bobbins diagonally. The details show how to divide the threads round the uppermost pin. They will not slip if you secure them near the pin.

Another way of inserting gimp.

Fig. 9–14. This can sometimes be done without a twist, as here. Insert gimp into different pairs but without a twist. See laces on pp. 53 and 58.

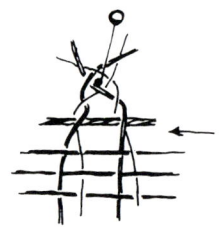

Cloth stitch ground

Fig. 9–15. Cloth stitch ground. This is done with whole stitches, twisting the pairs as they turn round the pins.

Cane ground

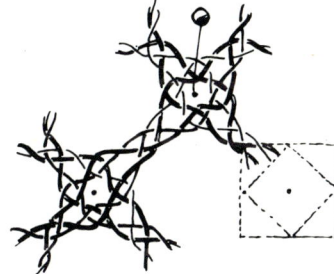

Fig. 9–17. Cane ground: Double stitch. (The digits in the inset indicate the order of the pairs.)

Pin-hole ground

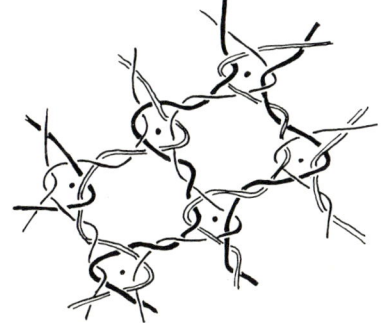

Brabant ground

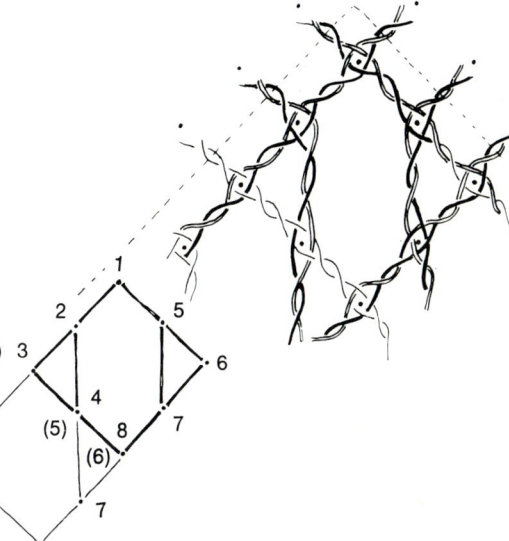

Fig. 9–16. Brabant ground. Follow this procedure: Half-stitch, twist, pin, half-stitch, twist. (The digits in the inset indicate the order of the pairs.)

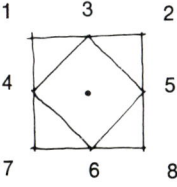

Fig. 9–18. Pin-hole ground. Follow this procedure: Half-stitch, twist, pin, half-stitch, twist.

Tally

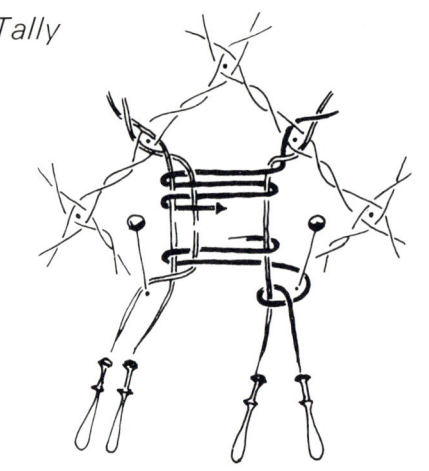

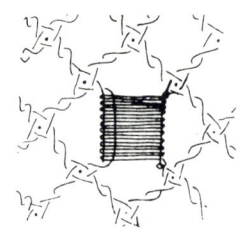

Fig. 9–19. Tally. A tally is made with two pairs of bobbins but only one twist. Stretch vertically on three of the bobbins. Fasten the furthest thread to the uppermost pair with the fourth bobbin, then turn round, passing alternately forwards and backwards, over and under the stretched threads. The stitches should be closed and tight with straight edges. (Be sure to use enough supporting pins.)

Separate pins

Fig. 9–22. Separate pins. Place the pins obliquely in the bottom of the ground with strong yarn to get a beautiful outline.

Finishing-off

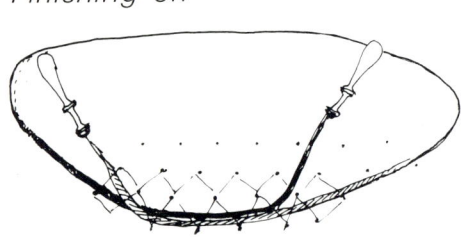

Fig. 9–20. Finishing-off with coarse threads that pass round each other.

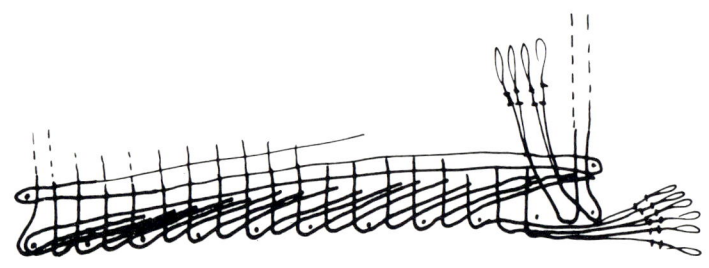

Fig. 9–21. Finishing-off with closed braid. Pin the six threads to the lace. Take the workers moving over the passives from left to right out to the furthest pin to the right. Twist the workers, then turn a whole stitch, and return through four pairs. Remove one pair

from the lace, but do not cut the threads until you have finished-off the entire pattern. The following two passives on the right side lie between the first and second pin-holes. Twist the workers, pass with a whole stitch through the next four pairs, and remove one of them. For the third passive, twist the workers, place a pin in the second pin-hole, and make whole stitches to the pin and through four pairs. Follow this procedure for the rest of the passives. Fasten the three last pairs on the right to the lace with a needle. Cut the threads, leaving 2–4 in. (5–10 cm.). Cut the remaining threads close while the pins are still in the pattern.

Joining edges

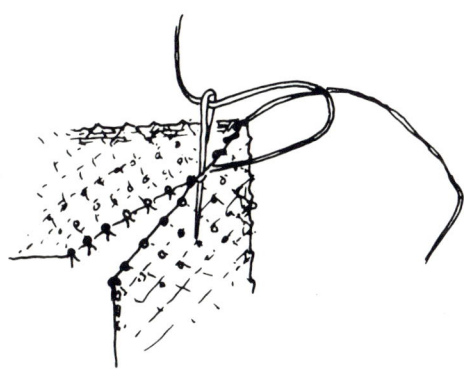

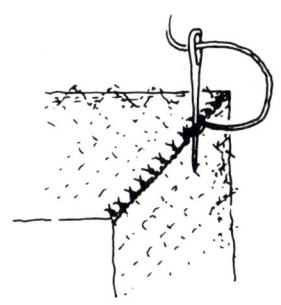

Fig. 9–23. Joining edges. Beginning from the upper side, leave half the thread, place the entire border on top of the corner threads, and sew in the pin-holes.

Fig. 9–24. Inside. Cast-off the corner stitches tightly with the thread remaining from the previous step.

Hem-stitch

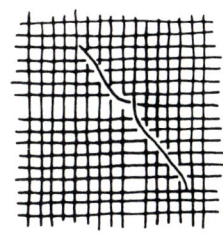

a.

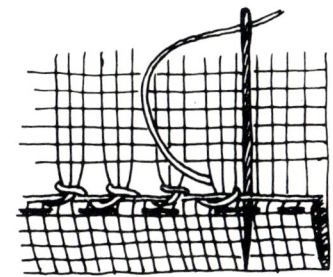

b.

Fig. 9–25. Hem-stitch. This should be used in most cases to finish-off a hem neatly. a. Draw out one thread. b. Then tack round three threads.

How to sew corners

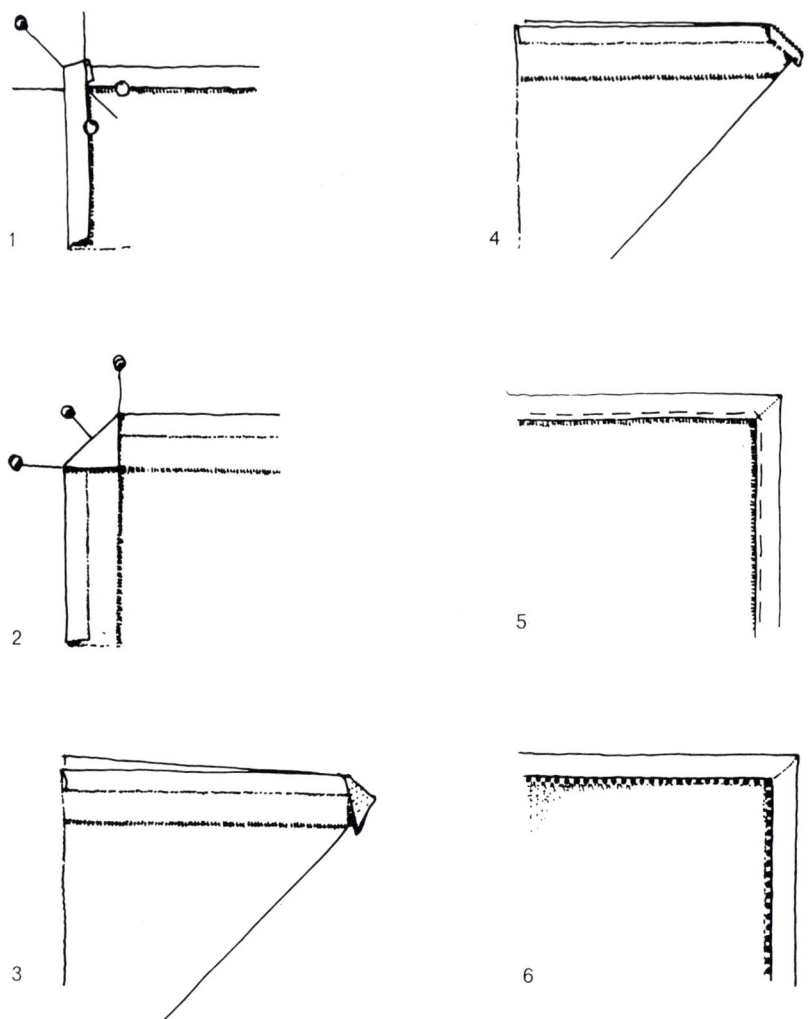

Fig. 9–26. How to sew corners. 1. Fold a hem on the linen cloth. Put three pins in the folded corners, one in the corner itself and the others where the hems meet, one in each hem. 2. Fold the corner into a triangle pointing inward. The pins will form a straight line. 3. Double the triangle backwards. The corner pin will be in the point and the other two will cover each other. Sew the edges together with small stitches, and remove the pins. 4. Fold the triangle upward, and cut away the surplus linen. 5. Fold the hem back to its original position, and tack it. 6. Hem-stitch.

How to stitch a bag

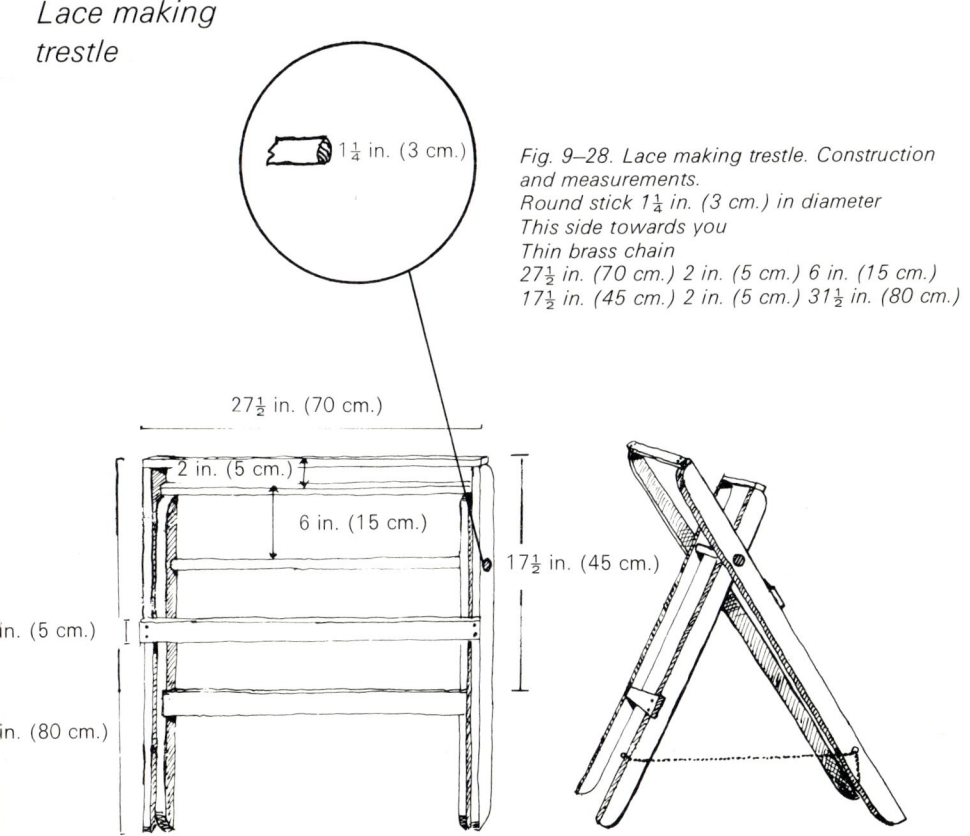

Fig. 9–27. How to stitch a bag (such as the carrier bag in Chapter 8). a. Cut out a suitably large piece of fabric, and hem the upper edge. Double the fabric with the inner *side out, and sew it together to form a bag. b. Sew the corners down to make the bag square. c. Turn the bag inside-out again, and sew on the handles.*

Lace making trestle

1¼ in. (3 cm.)

Fig. 9–28. Lace making trestle. Construction and measurements.
Round stick 1¼ in. (3 cm.) in diameter
This side towards you
Thin brass chain
27½ in. (70 cm.) 2 in. (5 cm.) 6 in. (15 cm.)
17½ in. (45 cm.) 2 in. (5 cm.) 31½ in. (80 cm.)

27½ in. (70 cm.)

2 in. (5 cm.)

6 in. (15 cm.)

17½ in. (45 cm.)

in. (5 cm.)

in. (80 cm.)

Fig. 3–17. Pattern drawing in full scale.
See photograph, page 35.

Fitting a square-shaped bracket lamp

This is a general instruction for fitting this type of lamp. The measurements given are those for 'Gallery bracket lamp' in Chapter 5.
Measurements: 8 in. (19·2 cm.) high; 6 in. (14·4 cm.) wide; $3\frac{3}{4}$ in. (9 cm.) deep.
Material: 10 in. (24 cm.) semi-bleached linen; 14 in. (33·6 cm.) lining; 32 in. (76·8 cm.) cotton ribbon; lamp frame; cotton thread.
Procedure: Stretch the lining round the frame from the inside and round the linen from the outside. Wind cotton ribbons round the stay marked with an A in the sketch, fig. 9–29. You do not have to wind the stay at C with ribbons because it is hidden between the linen and the lining.

Cut the linen fabric into strips $\frac{3}{4}$ in. (1·8 cm.) wide, and fold them. Wind them tightly round the stay with the folded edge covering the cut edge. Finish by folding the ribbons round the stay marked B, and stitch them together.

Pin on the lining from inside the covered stay. Stitch it together closely, and cut off the unravelled threads. The stitches will be on the outside of the frame, covered by the linen.

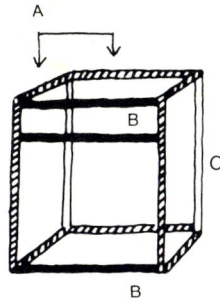

Fig. 9–29. Fitting a bracket lamp.

Pin the lace on the linen, and hem-stitch on both sides round three threads. Fasten the lace invisibly at the upper and lower edges. Press the linen with a damp cloth, but do not touch the lace.

Pin the linen and the lace on the frame. Fold straight round it, allowing $\frac{1}{4}$ in. (6 mm.) for the seam. Adjust the lace edge so that the hem-stitching will follow the stay in a straight line. Fasten the linen to the lining with small stitches.

Suppliers

Great Britain

Mace & Nairn, 89 Crane St., Salisbury, Wilts., SP1 2PY sell bobbins, and linen yarn.

The Needlewoman Shop, 146 Regent St., London W.1 sell bobbins, and cotton and linen yarn.

Christine Riley, 53 Barclay St., Stonehaven, Kincardineshire, AB3 2AR sell bobbins, and cotton yarn.

No manufacturer or importer of lace pillows in Great Britain can at present be traced. It is hoped that this situation will soon be remedied, but in the meantime readers are recommended to make their own pillows.

United States

Some Place, 2990 Adeline St., Berkeley, Calif. 94703 sell a basic bobbin lace kit.

Berga/Ullman, Box 831, Ossining, New York, N.Y. 10562 sell a traditional Swedish padded lace pillow, bobbins etc.

Yarn Center, 866 Avenue of the Americas, New York, N.Y. sell a wide variety of yarns.

Robin and Russ Handweavers, 533 North Adams Street, McMinniville, Oregon 97128 sell a wide variety of yarns.

Merribee Needlecraft Company, 2904 West Lancaster, Fort Worth, Texas 76107 sell yarns by mail order, also have a number of retail shops.

Frederick J. Fawcett, Inc., 129 South Street, Boston, Mass. 02111 sell all kinds of linen yarn.